INDIRA GANDHI AND HER POWER GAME

Indira Gandhi and Her Power Game

Janardan Thakur

VIKAS PUBLISHING HOUSE PVT LTD
VIKAS HOUSE, 20/4 Industrial Area, Sahibabad
Distt. Ghaziabad, U.P. (India)

VIKAS PUBLISHING HOUSE PVT LTD
VIKAS HOUSE, 20/4 Industrial Area, Sahibabad, Distt. Ghaziabad
Branches : Savoy Chambers, 5 Wallace Street, Bombay / 10 First
Main Road, Gandhi Nagar, Bangalore / 8/1-B Chowringhee Lane,
Calcutta / 80 Canning Road, Kanpur

ISBN 0-7069-0985-2

1V2T1303

First impression, 1979
Second impression, 1979

To
my Brothers and Sisters

Printed at The Central Electric Press, 80-D, Kamla Nagar, Delhi 110007

PREFACE

After I had finished writing *All the Prime Minister's Men* in July 1977, I had shoved all my notes and clippings on Mrs Gandhi into a large envelope, sealed it with cellotape and consigned it to the bottom of my filing cabinet, hoping it would never have to be brought out again, except to be thrown. How wrong I was! Within months half my reporter's notebooks were full of her, and for every new clippings file on all the Janata men put together, there were at least three on Mrs Gandhi alone. She was not just still there, she was bang in the centre of the political stage. She was like the Maypole, with crowds dancing round her, never mind if most of them were only clamouring for her blood. It all helped her.

Mrs Gandhi's excesses had given birth to the Janata Party, and now the pendulum seemed to be swinging back to her. She was once again being hailed as the only person who could restore order and discipline in the country, and obviously many were only too ready to fall in the trap again—the trap of her "charismatic leadership." What was all her charisma about? What did she have to give to the country? Nobody has seen her from a closer range as Prime Minister than P.N. Haksar, who was largely responsible for creating all the mystique of her greatness, and if you want his assessment of the lady, he would tell you there is "nothing in her—no substance, no conviction." All that is necessary is the initial success in seizing power and the total control of all means of propaganda to project a leader as a supernatural figure. And what has smoothed the path of many a dictator is a lack of political judgment on the part of a dissatisfied, embittered people who are ready to surrender themselves to the redeemer cult.

It is not just the bumbling leaders of the Janata Party who helped the lady on her come-back drive. We have all done it. When I began writing this book, I asked many of my friends in the press what they thought of the way the media had treated Mrs Gandhi during the last 28 months. The reply that came from a friend summed it up: "The media was obsessed with Mrs Gandhi. Indian newsmen follow her as the Englishmen do their Queen. They think she is good copy. This may be so, but most media men somehow unconsciously give her more exposure than she deserves. They do not use their critical faculties to assess her past, present and future. Those who are in authority, people who are responsible for edit pages, have not been able to evaluate the potential threat emanating from her camp to democratic institutions in this country. This could be for two reasons. One, most newsmen in this country have vested interests in the sense that they support one party or the other. And secondly, at the back of their mind those who oppose her fear that she may come back to power and they may either lose their jobs or opportunities for advancement. Senior journalists aspire for either foreign office postings or appointments to political offices. Such desire cannot make them free agents to comment at will objectively. When a leader writer sits down in front of a typewriter he always looks behind his shoulders and wonders what if she came back to power? His opinions are dictated by this paranoia."

Let me confess, I too have been obsessed with Mrs Gandhi. I have certainly written more on her than on any other individual. But to the best of my ability, I have tried to see her as she truly is. And that is what this book is about.

Before I leave you to it, I must thank all my friends and colleagues who helped and encouraged me in the project. I must also thank Avinash Pasricha, Pramod Pushkarna, Mandira Purie, Krishna Murari Kishan, Girija Shankar Singh, Madan Malhotra, Rajendra Sareen, Vijay Vashishta, Pana India and Focus for providing the photographs in this book.

I owe a very special debt of gratitude to my wife and children without whose prodding and help this book would have taken ages to write.

JANARDAN THAKUR

CONTENTS

I

THE LADY IN TEARS

It was like no other night before. Hardly anybody slept. They were out on the streets, in cities and towns, from one end of the country to the other. Even in villages little knots of people were glued around any available radio set.

The night of 20 March 1977, stunningly joyous for the victors, cataclysmic for the vanquished.

Delhi was incredibly jubilant. Well past midnight the crowds still surged round the high billboards set up for the election results. Bahadur Shah Zafar Marg, all the way down from the Tilak bridge, was jammed with cars and scooters and people. Some had brought out their drums, some their bugles. Wild cheers went up with every hated name that fell by the wayside, reminiscent of that other night in December 1971 when the Lahore skies had belonged to India. Those were the days when so many had hailed Indira Gandhi as Durga. Now she was down in the dumps. Suddenly, all too suddenly, the power and the glory had passed.

The overarching sky was all that seemed common that night between the rest of the city and the house that had been the centre of power for eleven long years. No. 1 Safdarjang Road lay wrapped in silence, a silence you could cut with a knife. Not even the dogs, the two Irish Wolfhounds, barked when Pupul Jayakar,[1] a

[1]Pupul Jayakar was then the Chairman of the All India Handicrafts Board.

friend of Mrs Gandhi for over 30 years, reached the house around 9 p.m. No cars crowded the entrance, no bustle of people. Mrs Jayakar was shown straight to the sitting room. Mrs Gandhi was alone, lost in thoughts. She smiled when she saw her friend, got up and embraced her.

"Pupul, I have lost," she said.

Mrs Jayakar had known that Indira was trailing behind, but the finality of that statement left her nonplussed. "Are you sure, Indira?" she asked. Mrs Gandhi just nodded. They were together for the next three hours, but neither said very much. Silence was communication enough between the two. Indira's face, Mrs Jayakar felt, was stoic in its passivity. "There was in her a still courage, a strange inward dignity. . . ." She had of course no way of gauging Mrs Gandhi's thoughts. Memories of the past? Forebodings of the future? Or could it be that her thoughts were with her son, trailing his dusty course back from Sultanpur.

After his defeat became certain, Sanjay Gandhi and his wife had driven back to Lucknow, escorted by a dozen toughs. At the residence of his faithful crony, Chief Minister Narain Dutt Tewari, Sanjay had shuttled frantically for hours between the teleprinter room and his special suite.[2] He looked a wreck. Flipping through the ticker reports desperately, he had asked one of the officers, "How is mummy?" The news that she too was trailing behind left him stunned. Around 11 p.m., he and his wife took a special plane back to Delhi.

Only a few days before the elections, Mrs Gandhi had a premonition that she would lose. It was not the reports of the Research and Analysis Wing (RAW) or the Information Bureau which bothered her. Nor the veiled hints in newspaper reports that her party was in for a debacle. Hadn't these prophets of gloom been proved wrong before? Hadn't they forecast a defeat for her in 1971? What had worried her was the sudden snapping of a *rudrakshamala* given to her by her spiritual guru, Ma Anandamayee. She had hurriedly gathered the beads, but they were fewer than before. She could not find the missing ones. She had taken it as an ominous sign.

Oh lord! why hadn't she listened to Sanjay Gandhi? He had been so insistent that she should not go to the polls. So was Bansi Lal,

[2]*Indian Express*, 21 March 1977.

her Defence Minister. Between them, Sanjay and Bansi Lal had even chalked out a plan of action. They wanted a constituent assembly as a first step towards it. They had even lobbied for it, supposedly without her consent, and many of their cronies in high places were willing to go along with them. A document entitled "A fresh look at our Constitution" was already in circulation. It sought to alter the Constitution to establish a Gaullist style presidential system and a "Superior Council of the Judiciary" which would supercede the authority of the Supreme Court. It was obviously a fruit of their annoying experiences with the country's existing judicial system. Mrs Gandhi herself had been convinced about the need for a change in the Constitution, but she was not sure if she could carry it through even in her own party. The storm of protest that the proposals met with, in spite of the Emergency and the gagged Press, weakened her. In the spirit of a true democrat, she had declared that "these decisions have to be taken by the people of the country as a whole."[3] She had allowed the plan to fizzle out. Was it not a mistake ?

If such were the thoughts that went through her mind that night, her face had not given her away. Her Special Envoy, Mohammad Yunus, had walked in with an anguished face, looking haggard and distraught. Her personal aide, R.K. Dhawan, was ashen-faced as he brought in a slip, obviously the latest figures from Rae Bareli, which was on a hot line. She took it calmly and invited Pupul Jayakar to join her for dinner. Where were Rajiv and Sonia? She was told they did not feel like having dinner. But they *must*, she insisted. Sonia, her Italian daughter-in-law, came wiping her eyes. Rajiv followed quietly, looking greatly disturbed. "They sat fiddling with some fruit," recorded Mrs Jayakar later. But Mrs Gandhi never lost her composure, not even when Dhawan entered again to tell her that the lead over her had mounted to 25,000. Without waiting for further details, she had summoned a Cabinet meeting.

When Mrs Jayakar left around midnight, the ministers had started arriving. A vital decision had to be taken. The Emergency must be revoked before it was too late. She feared that it might be used against her; some of her advisers had told her so. She must withdraw the Emergency fast. And so the midnight Cabinet meeting.

[3]*The Far Eastern Economic Review*, 16 January 1976.

She had not bothered about the Cabinet when she clamped the Emergency, but now she was going about it in a proper way, lest somebody questioned the validity of the withdrawal. She was assailed by all sorts of fears, but her face never showed the inner turmoil.

Her Cabinet colleagues, whom she had been used to treating as a bunch of errand boys, were amazed at her courtesy and sweetness that night. In an unusual gesture she had gone out to the portico to bid them goodbye. This is how Khwaja Ahmed Abbas, who went around for months diligently picking the pieces of that eventful day, put the scene together:

When the last car drove away, she was left standing alone and went into the house that (she suddenly remembered) she had now no right to call her own . . . Outside, there was the shuffling of the security guard's boots and the metallic click of his rifle as he shifted position from "attention" to "at ease." "*Koi hai!*" she called out to her servants. There was no one . . . She went towards the telephone and picked it up. "Yes, Ma'm," answered the sleepy voice of the operator. "Shall I get you Rae Bareli?" How did he know? she wondered. "No," she replied aloud. "Get me Om Mehta," She knew that he had quicker ways of contacting Rae Bareli . . . .[4]

By 3 a.m. on 21 March all the world knew about the end of another Raj. All attempts of Mrs Gandhi's election agent at Rae Bareli, Fotedar, to force a decision for a re-poll, or at least a recount in order to stall the announcement of the result, had failed. Even the Prime Minister's principal factotum, Yashpal Kapoor, who had earned for himself the title of "Prince of Rae Bareli" could not do a thing beyond pacing up and down the court room, now phoning Om Mehta in New Delhi, now dialling the Chief Minister and the Chief Secretary in Lucknow and now the Home Secretary Khurana in Delhi. The young District Magistrate, Vinod Malhotra, refused to be pressurized and went ahead with the official announcement. "For Shrimati Indira Nehru Gandhi," he read out, "one lakh, twentytwo thousand, five hundred and seventeen . . . Shri Raj Narain, one lakh, seventyseven thousand, seven hundred and nineteen. *Nirvachit.*"

[4]In his book, 20th March 1977.

Mrs Gandhi decided she would retire for the night.

Later that morning she had come out looking somewhat confused and ill at ease. To one visitor it had seemed she was not sure how to behave in the changed circumstances. But as her party colleagues came in one by one to reaffirm their faith in her, she gradually felt more herself. Her eyes fell on G.S. Dhillon and Raj Bahadur standing there with folded hands. How reassuring to hear them say that she alone could save the Congress! The Congress President, Dev Kant Barooah, had seemed a little less deferential than before, but was saying the right things, whether he meant them or not. "The country needs you, you should remain in politics . . .." She was taking in every word, every glance, assessing each one of them. "The rats will leave the sinking ship," Sanjay had warned her.[5] His words mattered much more to her now. She was going to be careful, watch every step she took.

Before she went over to the Acting President, B.D. Jatti, to hand over her resignation on 22 March, she summoned her last Cabinet meeting. Her colleagues, many of whom had themselves been bulldozed by the electorate, placed on record their "deep appreciation" of her "outstanding services." She herself made her first post-resignation pronouncement as nice and humble as possible: "The collective judgment of the people must be respected. My colleagues and I accept their verdict unreservedly and in a spirit of humility." And like a true democrat she went on to offer to the new government her "constructive cooperation." "The stout-hearted heroine of many a political upheaval in India's modern history who succumbed in the last battle of the ballot she fought was serene and dignified as she went through the motions of winding up the last vestiges of her 11-year historic and deeply controversial rule," wrote an emotionally-surcharged correspondent.[6]

It sounded as though she were going to retire from politics,—at least for some time—and indeed that was the impression she gave to many. She was vague about her plans. She had not even decided, she told some of her colleagues, where she was going to live or how she was going to make a living. That was exactly what she told a

---

[5]*India Today*, 1-15 September 1977.
[6]A.N. Dar in *Indian Express*, 23 March 1977.

correspondent a couple of weeks later.[7] She was still "house-hunting" and there was a lot of packing to be done. To some colleagues and supporters she talked vaguely about withdrawing for some months to some Ashram or some quiet retreat in Dehra Dun. And as though to show to the world that she was genuinely hard up for funds, the word was diligently spread around that an industrial house had offered to meet her household expenses.

Her posture of withdrawal was a studied one. It was a ruse to draw out the intentions of her party colleagues, to know where each one of them stood. She had lost the government, but would not lose her hold over the party at any cost. Knowing the stuff her partymen were made of she was pretty certain that very few would have the guts to challenge her leadership. She had already spotted her enemies, especially the ones who had been attacking her son. "An attack on Sanjay is an attack on me," she had declared long before. That was even more true now. She would tolerate anyone but a Sanjay-baiter.

One of them was Subhadra Joshi. She had for long been a trusted friend of Mrs Gandhi, but the day she became a critic of Sanjay Gandhi's activities during the Emergency she brought on herself the wrath of his mother. But now that Mrs Gandhi was defeated, Mrs Joshi had felt a surge of sympathy for her. She wanted to go and convey her sorrow, if only for old time's sake. She mustered courage and went.[8] She had barely been ushered into a room when Mrs Gandhi breezed in, a frown on her face. For a while she just stood there without a word. Then Subhadra Joshi ventured: "Can I sit down?"

"Sit down," replied Mrs Gandhi curtly. Both sat down, at quite a distance from each other.

Since Mrs Gandhi was saying not a word, not even asking why she had come, Mrs Joshi ventured again: "I just came to say how sorry I am about your defeat."

"I am sick of insincerity," said Mrs Gandhi coldly.

"Believe me, I am genuinely pained...."

"Was that why you stabbed me in the back?" Mrs Gandhi asked with sarcasm.

That was an unexpected charge. Subhadra Joshi could guess what Mrs Gandhi was driving at. Only a day before, Mrs Joshi and

[7]*The Statesman*, 7 April 1977.
[8]Subhadra Joshi in an interview with the author.

some of her like-minded friends had raised the demand that the Congress President should inquire into the "misdeeds" of the Youth Congress and other members of the Sanjay caucus and punish all those responsible for the party's debacle. Obviously Mrs Gandhi had kept a close watch on who was doing what.

"I do think it was suicidal for you to tolerate Bansi Lal and company..."

She was cut short by Mrs Gandhi. "What can be more insulting to me," she fumed, "than the suggestion that I had been doing whatever Bansi Lal and others wanted me to do?"

"To harm you or the party has never been my motive," said Mrs Joshi.

"I don't know your motive," Mrs Gandhi replied impatiently. "Whatever you are doing is okay." And with a curt *"Namaste"* she breezed out of the room.

Subhadra Joshi and her colleague, Desh Raj Goel,[9] had gone round meeting Dev Kant Barooah, Brahmanand Reddi, C. Subramaniam and other senior leaders of the party, telling them that they and the party must state clearly that Mrs Gandhi and the Sanjay caucus had been responsible for the electoral rout. But they found these leaders either vacillating or gutless. Courtiers and chattels of the lady, they were faceless men who had lost their identities long ago. Much as some of them criticized her in their drawing rooms, some even hurling invectives at her, most of them secretly desired her favour and support. "Well, we are all guilty..." they mumbled to Joshi and Goel. Even Y.B. Chavan was cautious and evasive. He had already received the hint from Mrs Gandhi that she would support him for the leadership of the Congress Parliamentary Party. The post carried the status of a minister and the possibility that at some point in the future he might be called upon to form a government. There was not a chance in sight, but it was a possibility all the same.

Mrs Joshi and her friend were getting nowhere. Nobody seemed willing to bell the cat. But surely if they avoided a direct reference to the lady and concentrated on the caucus the move would get support, they thought. On 21 March they wrote out a petition to

[9] D.R. Goel, a former AICC member, in an interview with the author.

the Congress President asking for an inquiry to find the guilty men. They went around looking for signatures, but only a few seemed willing to sign the petition. K.L. Shrimali, who had resigned the vice-chancellorship of Benares Hindu University to contest the Lok Sabha elections and lost, Mir Mushtaq, Chairman of the Delhi Metropolitan Council, O.P. Bahl, an Executive Councillor, and a few others agreed. None of the so-called stalwarts of the party agreed. "Barooah was saying she (Mrs Gandhi) was responsible for the defeat but he was not prepared to make a statement. In fact, Swaran Singh was the only person who was holding his own, not defending her."[10]

The very next day, the first post-election meeting of the Congress Working Committee was held. Mrs Gandhi's arrival had been preceded by the usual flutter. She had the same sprightly walk, the same smile for waiting cameramen. "I have no special plans," she had told the waiting reporters. "I will continue to work for the party."[11] She was still the Prime Minister, seven hours after resignation.

Though unsure of the posture that the party would adopt towards her, she kept her studied poise. All others were still in a state of daze, not knowing what course to take. Used to being driven by the lady for years, they fell in line almost automatically. She saw it happening and knew, she was still the master. Not a shade of remorse or contrition did her words have. Instead, she virtually laid the blame on the organisation. Nobody challenged her. The Working Committee promptly placed on record its "deep appreciation and admiration for the outstanding leadership of Mrs Gandhi to the party and the nation as Prime Minister" and hoped that "she will continue to lead us." Declared the still-faithful Purabi Mukherjee: "Mrs Gandhi continues to be our leader."

Even so, the Congress Working Committee had taken a decision which had angered Mrs Gandhi. It had asked for a "detailed analysis" of the factors responsible for the electoral debacle. She could see the threat involved; a detailed analysis could show her up as the main culprit. She could easily guess who was behind the move. Chandrajeet Yadav, one of the many fake leftists in the

[10]*Ibid.*
[11]*The Statesman*, 23 March 1977.

party, had demanded organisational elections to democratise the party's functioning. The man was obviously in league with Barooah. Immediately the lady's hatchetman, Bansi Lal, was up in arms. "What is the need for organisational elections?" he shouted. "It can wait till the State Assembly elections." But Yadav had done his homework. He had many behind him. He even got the Congress Working Committee to agree to a three-day debate on the debacle from 12 April.

Mrs Gandhi was furious. Barooah must be ousted. And so she set loose her faithful hounds. Satpal Kapoor, an old faithful, Raja Dinesh Singh who had been itching to be back in the fold, A.P. Sharma and several others were out to draw Barooah's blood. They demanded the collective resignation of all the Congress Working Committee members, including the President. Masterminding the operation were Bansi Lal and Sanjay Gandhi. They knew what was coming. The former Defence Minister had already received a letter from Barooah asking him to quit the Congress Working Committee. The cheek of that court jester! He had even sent marching orders to Narain Dutt Tewari, another nominated member of the Working Committee. His intentions were obvious. The next attack would be on Sanjay, if not on Mrs Gandhi herself.

Sanjay Gandhi was in no doubt about the humiliation that awaited him. The new leaders of the country had declared they would probe the Maruti scandal. He knew he would be attacked by the very people who till recently compared him to Vivekananda and Sankaracharya. Barooah was already calling him a "Borstal character." At least he wouldn't allow that joker the chance to throw him out of the AICC. Promptly he announced to the Press that he was quitting "active politics." That was merely a prelude to the resignation he was soon going to send Barooah. More as a postscript to his announcement, the Emergency hero had added: "I am all the more sorry if what I did in my personal capacity has recoiled on my mother..." Such feelings of guilt or remorse were even more alien to Sanjay than to his mother. But the plea that what he had done was in his "personal capacity" was a studied excuse for the future.

The other strongman of the Emergency, Bansi Lal, had gone running to Mrs Gandhi for help against the attacks he was facing. She could ditch her Goebbels, V.C. Shukla, but she could hardly afford to let Bansi Lal down. To do that would mean trouble for herself. Even otherwise she was becoming increasingly apprehensive. Some of the Janata leaders, especially George Fernandes, had been spewing venom against her and all sorts of rumours were afloat about how Sanjay Gandhi would be dealt with. He was her weakest spot, her Achilles' heel, as even her aunt, Vijaya Lakshmi Pandit had remarked.

Within a day of Morarji Desai becoming the Prime Minister, Mrs Gandhi had run to him to seek mercy for her son. "Do anything but save his life," she pleaded. She knew she was in a spot. And yet, even her own partymen appeared to be going over to the devil. Even that "ungrateful" Y.B. Chavan whom she had put in the Opposition leader's seat had told the Lok Sabha in his opening speech that the Congress had learnt its lessons from the elections and had "bid goodbye to Emergency for good." He had sounded more like saying goodbye to Mrs Gandhi than to the Emergency. When his speech was reported to Mrs Gandhi that evening, she had gone red with anger. She knew there had to be a battle at home, too.

On 31 March she manoeuvred an informal meeting of the CWC at her residence. Among those who came were Barooah, Chavan, C. Subramaniam, Swaran Singh, Brahmanand Reddi and Siddhartha Shankar Ray. None of them seemed to know what it was all about until Mrs Gandhi came out with her cards. She told them she had passed on the resignation letter of Bansi Lal to Y.B. Chavan but it would be given to Barooah only if all the CWC members including the President resigned. Chavan, Reddi and Subramaniam seemed willing to go along with her suggestion, but Swaran Singh, Ray and Mir Qasim thought it was wrong to equate everybody with the caucus.

She then threw her trump card. "I'll quit the party if Bansi Lal or anybody is singled out for action."

The threat worked. All the stalwarts fell in line once again. But the triumph was short-lived. A stormy petrel from Kerala, Vayalar Ravi, shot up to declare that he would not be equated with the caucus. "This meeting here has no locus standi. It can't undo what the Working Committee has formally done."

That gave new strength to Barooah. He nodded assent. "It is a moment of truth for the Congress. We must have a free and frank debate." The lady's gambit had failed. But she wasn't giving up so easily. She would now try another tactic: cajole Barooah. Mohammad Yunus, now her personal Special Envoy, was sent to Barooah to make peace. When he failed, Mrs Gandhi sent her special private secretary, R.K. Dhawan, to invite the Congress President over to her house. Barooah went, but he stuck to his guns. He had kept quiet when she told him she would not go to the Congress Working Committee meeting on 12 April. Perhaps she expected he would implore her to come. But then the times had changed, and how!

Barooah had gone ahead with his plans. He had even invited all the Congress Chief Ministers, the PCC chiefs and the former Central Ministers, making it almost a mini-AICC. Mrs Gandhi had grown desperate. She feared that even her party was slipping from her grasp. Pushed back to the wall, her defence mechanism had come into full play. Gone was that initial pose of humility. She had started defending her son aggressively, on every occasion. It was an oversimplification to blame Sanjay Gandhi or Bansi Lal for the party's election debacle, she said in the first interview she gave after her defeat.[12] "Bansi Lal may have done something in Haryana, but he certainly wasn't responsible for anything else... And so far as I know, Sanjay stuck just to his five points..." The defeat, she said blandly, was only due to "a massive propaganda campaign." She had only now learnt of the intensity and virulence of the propaganda made by the former Opposition parties. She refuted suggestions that she took decisions without her Cabinet colleagues. Nothing happened behind the scenes. But having said so, she had an after-thought: she admitted she had not consulted her Cabinet on two occasions—the devaluation of the rupee and the proclamation of the Emergency. She had no regrets, no repentance. And of course she was totally unimpressed by the zeal displayed by some of her colleagues now rushing on to the anti-Sanjay bandwagon. "They should have spoken of their misgivings earlier instead of trumpeting them now..."

"Expel me, expel me," Mrs Gandhi cried hysterically when the Congress Working Committee decided to expel Bansi Lal unless he resigned from the primary membership within 12 hours.

She knew these leaders could not go beyond finding scapegoats for the debacle. They could not touch her. She had shown the

[12]*The Statesman*, 7 April 1977.

world that they could not even hold a meeting by themselves. The day before, on 12 April, she had not turned up for the opening session of the Congress Working Committee meeting. Even before they could start the proceedings there was a well-orchestrated chorus demanding her presence. Sitaram Kesari, one of the cronies from Bihar, had ensured that. Barooah sought to explain that he had personally tried to persuade her to come but she had chosen to stay away. "No, no, we cannot go on without her," Kesari and some others had shouted. The stalwarts— Barooah, Chavan and Tripathi—put their heads together in hurried consultation. Next moment all three were out in the portico. "Staging a walk-out?" a surprised reporter had asked.[13] How could they be leaving so soon? "No, we are going to Mrs Gandhi," the monocled Barooah said. He was tense and glum.

They had found her all dressed and ready but unwilling to go to the meeting. "But the members are clamouring for you, you must come," the three leaders pleaded. Saying no, no, she consented.

Bugles were sounded as she arrived. "*Desh ki Neta Indira Gandhi*" shouted the Youth Congress workers. They looked anything but youths. Only that morning they had started a fast at the gate to demand Barooah's ouster. Whether planned or not, Mrs Gandhi had stolen the thunder.

With a well-timed masterly stroke she had already blunted the knives sharpened for her dear ones. Just the night before the meeting she had sent off a cleverly drafted letter to Barooah. "I should like to make it clear," she wrote, "that as one who led the Government, I unreservedly own full responsibility for this defeat. I am not interested in finding alibis or excuses for myself, nor am I interested in shielding anyone. I have no caucus to defend or group to fight. I have never functioned as a faction leader...."

The brain behind this pre-emptive strategy was none other than D.P. Mishra who had played her Chanakya during the Congress split of 1969. "By doing this you would be turning the tables on Barooah and others," Mishra had advised. The letter had not quite assuaged the feelings of Mrs Gandhi's detractors, but it certainly took the wind out of their sails. Now that she had owned the full responsibility herself and denied the very existence of a caucus what could they do? Could they ask for her expulsion from the party or demand that she be reprimanded?

[13]Vijay Sanghvi in *Sandesh*, 13 April 1977.

A reprimand would have been perfectly in order, thought K.P. Unnikrishnan,[14] the articulate M.P. from Kerala, known for his leftist leanings. He had been a voluble supporter of Mrs Gandhi until it became difficult for him to take her imperious style. He had no doubt the party had blundered right in the beginning, on 22 March, when it rushed into reaffirming its faith in her leadership.

Unnikrishnan claimed he was the first to have gone hammer and tongs at the lady when some of the Congressmen met at the house of Chandrajeet Yadav a few days after the election results. If the party were to survive it must change its ways, he said. It must find out why it had suffered such an ignominious defeat, never mind whether Mrs Gandhi liked it or not. Her leadership was exhausted, she had nothing worthwhile to offer. Nobody ever had a chance like her's, not even Nehru. When he began in 1947, Nehru was beset with gigantic problems of nation building. He had inherited a ramshackle economy, chronic food deficits, a depleted army. But Mrs Gandhi had become a national heroine almost overnight. Suddenly in 1969 she was the symbol of a national resurgence. In 1971 she got an absolute mandate. Congressmen who had broken off from the Syndicate leaders because of their Tammany Hall style thought here was a leader who would create a new cadre-based party. They thought the days of bossism were over. What a surprise they were in for!

"We had all contributed our share to the development of the personality cult," conceded Dharambir Sinha who had been a member of Mrs Gandhi's Government. "But I had always thought that a leadership which was kept accountable would not deteriorate into a personality cult. In those days she had seemed to us a rejuvenator. The decay in her leadership qualities was a mysterious process, still an enigma to many of us."[15]

Unnikrishnan and some of his friends had lobbied hard to make the party assert itself. They had gone to Barooah, but found him vacillating, now blaming Mrs Gandhi and now her son. "What is the point in talking about Sanjay Gandhi," Unnikrishnan had told the Congress President. "Who was Sanjay? Was he an independent phenomenon? There is no use finding scapegoats."

[14]In an interview to the author.
[15]In an interview to the author.

Mrs Gandhi must not be allowed to escape the consequences of her actions, he had insisted.

But Barooah would not go that far, not openly at least. Of course he would do everything to expose the caucus, especially Sanjay Gandhi and Bansi Lal who had humiliated him during the Emergency. He knew his friend, Siddhartha Shankar Ray, would take care of Sanjay Gandhi, for he had his own bones to pick with the boy. As for that Jat bully, Barooah had worked hard on Banarsi Das Gupta, the man whom Bansi Lal had installed as the Chief Minister of Haryana when he himself was brought away to Delhi as Defence Minister. It had delighted Barooah to hear Bansi Lal being attacked by his own puppet. Banarsi Das had done it amazingly well, confessing that he had been a coward dancing to the tune of Bansi Lal. That very evening the CWC informally decided to expel Bansi Lal from the party.

Desperate to save Bansi Lal and her son, Mrs Gandhi had rushed to Barooah's house next morning. Barooah was again delighted: the queen had come to her jester's door for help. In what was said to have been a "very emotional" meeting, Mrs Gandhi assured him she did not want him to resign from presidentship. All she was asking for was to spare Sanjay and Bansi Lal from humiliation. They were already under attack from outside, why attack them in their home? Barooah would not say anything about Bansi Lal, but he gave his word that he would see to it that "Feroze Gandhi's son is not hurt."[16] After all, Feroze had been his bosom pal. He would certainly do this for his son. Sanjay Gandhi had promptly resigned from the AICC and the Working Committee members had discovered to their dismay that he had never been enrolled as a primary member of the party. What could they do except ridicule Barooah for having nominated the boy to the AICC? Not even did his friend, Siddhartha, spare him. "How could the President do such a thing?" he had demanded. Barooah adjusted his monocles and stayed mum.

He had kept his word, but if he thought Mrs Gandhi would live up to her assurance he still did not know her. The caucus hounds were still after him. Mrs Gandhi and her supporters knew that they could not capture the party without having a trusted man as President. Barooah could not be trusted. He was being used as a front by the enemies.

---

[16] Kewal Varma in *Business Standard*, 17 April 1977.

When Barooah finally quit, Mrs Gandhi wanted Brahmanand Reddi, her dumb Home Minister, to be the provisional President. But Barooah acted swiftly and proposed the name of Swaran Singh—his parting rebuff to Mrs Gandhi!

The war had only begun. New strategies were in the making. The next round was pure theatre, and very aptly the arena chosen for it was New Delhi's Mavalankar Hall, a favourite venue for stage plays, dance recitals and film shows. Here the Congressmen gathered in early May for their first AICC session after the party's defeat. The show began with a farcical skit on portraits—the "Battle of Portraits" as many named it.

The *dramatis personae* were taking their positions on the stage. Swaran Singh, the provisional president, was perched on two pillows, flanked by his general secretaries on one side and Y.B. Chavan and C. Subramaniam on the other. Brahmanand Reddi, the president-to-be, sat alone in the middle. D.P. Mishra, *Rishi*-like with his flowing white beard, squatted at the back of the stage. The lesser characters, and the "extras" sat mixed with the audience in the hall. Somebody saw the debonair V.C. Shukla slip on to the stage quietly and jeered, "What is that reprimanded man doing up there?" Shukla tarried for a while and then slunk away.

The deliberations were about to begin when suddenly the skit came on. B.P. Maurya, the volatile Harijan leader, shot up from his seat and shouted menacingly: *"Panditji ki tasveer kahan hai? Yeh sab chamchon ki karistani hai* (Where is the portrait of Panditji? All this is the doing of sycophants)." The cry was picked up by others. "Where is Mrs Gandhi's portrait?" somebody demanded. Shankar Dayal Singh, known for his corny sense of humour, shouted to Banarsi Das Gupta: "Why don't you ask for the portraits of Sanjay and Bansi Lal?" Cried a blunt Haryanvi: "How about a portrait of Raj Narain?"

General Secretary Purabi Mukherjee was up at the mike, trying hard to make herself heard. She was apologizing for the mistake. This had been the first AICC in years when the portraits of the father and the daughter were missing from the dais. By now, if all had gone well, Sanjay's portrait should have joined the pantheon. The times had changed, Purabi was reminding the clamorous lot shouting in the hall, but she was only referring to the sudden shift in the material situation of the AICC. Otherwise she was still very much a supporter of Mrs Gandhi.

About half an hour later large portraits of Jawaharlal and Indira Gandhi arrived, the daughter's far bigger than the father's. Flanked by the two, the Mahatma had suddenly shrunk in size. Indira's smiling face dominated the wall.

The lady herself was still to come. The consummate player that she was, her entry had to be dramatic, properly timed. She arrived on the crest of a surging crowd, right in the middle of Swaran Singh's drawling monotone, swamping his words. The flashing cameras, the throaty *zindabads*, the rush of excitement all around left her adversaries gaping.

She had just the right touch of sadness on her face when she came up to the mike, a little hesitantly, as though she were being pushed. She had not even wanted to come to the meeting, she began tremulously, but so many members from all over the country, from the South and the North (one could not miss her emphasis on the 'North') had pressed her to come that she couldn't avoid it. "I have only come to see you, and to thank you for the unstinted support you have given me. You have stood by me ...in good and bad times." And saying this she dissolved into tears and hurriedly withdrew from the stage, her exit as dramatic as her entry. "The pathetic figurine," one reporter had described her.

Mrs Gandhi gone, the salvo began. Speeches full of fire and brimstone. Some had probably been rehearsing for days, mustering courage to speak up. T.A. Pai had at last found his voice. He was holding forth on how the party had come to such a sorry pass. The debacle had started with the Chandigarh Congress session when efforts were made to project Sanjay Gandhi; the debacle was completed at Gauhati when efforts were made to substitute the Youth Congress for the Indian National Congress. Sanjay had become the leader of the Congress and a de facto authority in the Government, he had access to all files without any authority, he decided on promotions and appointments of ministers and terror was struck in the minds of the unobliging ones. Brave statements for a man who had himself played his part in boosting the Prime Minister's son or had succumbed to the pressures from the "palace" as he put it. "Now that we know the truth," Pai thundered, "are we prepared to go through the fire of purges?" Only retorts flew in from the other side. "If there was a caucus it was here," shouted M.V. Krishnappa, Karnataka M.P., pointing to Barooah sitting at the back of the stage. "This was the caucus," he repeated mockingly. Krishnappa could well have pointed to many others: Siddhartha Shankar Ray, Rajni Patel, Chandrajeet Yadav. They had themselves constituted one of Mrs Gandhi's recent caucuses. They had all been her back-room boys, without exception. Suddenly they were all full of courage, bursting with righteous indignation against Mrs Gandhi and her Sanjay caucus. What credibility could these cronies of yesterday have? It was all right until the lady was down and out, but how long could they hide their own worthlessness? The hollowness of her detractors was Mrs Gandhi's biggest strength.

In spite of all the strutting and fretting of her opponents, the lady's brief histrionics had carried the day for her. Tears had for long been a part of her repertoire. When her guiles and wiles failed, she wept. She had done it at least twice at the requisitioned AICC meeting in 1969 where she first split the party. And this was a time when she was going to spare none of her talents to get control over at least her own party.

Next day, 6 May, was the crucial election of the party President. There had been several men secretly aspiring for her support. Raja Dinesh Singh, a castaway courtier, was again trying hard to worm his way back into her grace in the hope that she might help him become the party chief. There was the prince of Kashmir who in his overweening ambition thought no other man would fit the chair better than him. Another serious aspirant was her confidant-turned-critic, Siddhartha Shankar Ray. He had gone over to the enemies the day he fell out with Sanjay Gandhi. Himself a co-architect of the Emergency, he had talked long and hard against the caucus which had displaced him at the court. He was now being projected by the "progressives" as the anti-Indira candidate for the presidency. But until the last few days, he had vacillated. Could he win without her support? The AICC was composed almost entirely of her handpicked men and he knew of the efforts she had made to get as many of her men to attend the meeting as she could. She had even sent out plane tickets to many of her AICC minions. No other leader in the party could beat her at resources. True, the pro-Communist lobby had worked hard to win over a sizeable chunk to their side, but could they stand up to her?

Ray was doubtful and had secretly gone to see Mrs Gandhi. Perhaps if I seek her blessings, he thought, she would be touched. And after all there are no permanent enemies or friends in politics.

Ray had returned with a rebuff. "What sort of Congressman are you?" Mrs Gandhi had rebuked. Didn't he realize that it was the South which had stood by the party? It was a matter of simple sense that the post should go to a man from the South. "I have already given my word to Brahmanand Reddi," she told Ray. "In fact Reddi should have been the Parliamentary Party leader. It was a mistake to choose Chavan." Chavan had already done enough to annoy Mrs Gandhi. She had decided she would no longer support anyone whom she could not trust fully. All these people had tried to act smart with her. Only Brahmanand Reddi had proved his worth as the Home Minister during the Emergency: he had shown that he had no mind of his own! He was the right man to back.

B. P. Maurya who was still to become her storm-trooper had been supporting Siddhartha for the presidentship. When Mrs Gandhi came to know of it, she called Maurya to her house.[17] Why was he supporting Ray? she asked him. Was it because of his brave fulminations against Sanjay Gandhi? Perhaps that is what had impressed him, she suggested. Maurya had not known what to say. After all, he had worked as a junior minister in her Government for so long. He did not want to be rude to her, not in her presence certainly. Mrs Gandhi went inside and returned with a letter. "Read this," she told Maurya. It was a letter to her from Siddhartha in which he had written effusively about Sanjay Gandhi, describing him as the "future hope of India." The letter had also condemned the CPI and the Russian lobby in the Congress which had started the Sanjay-baiting. "That is the brave man you are now supporting!" Mrs Gandhi had said with contempt. Maurya began working for the victory of Brahmanand Reddi.

The result seemed a foregone conclusion when the AICC members assembled the second day. It could be felt in the air, in the faces of those in the race. The Editor of a Calcutta Weekly[18] had asked Siddhartha Shankar Ray how things were. "How would I know?" he replied, highly strung. "You had better ask someone else." He looked harried, his eyes red without sleep. Anybody could tell he was a losing horse. Even the auditorium looked vastly different from the previous day. Instead of Barooah's Youth Congress President, Priyaranjan Das Munshi, there was Sanjay's Youth

[17] B.P. Maurya in an interview with the author.
[18] M.J. Akbar in *Sunday*.

Congress President, Janardan Singh Gehlot, "smiling from the dais." Outside the hall, too, the Sanjay goons predominated.

When Brahmanand Reddi was declared elected, the zindabads were all for Mrs Gandhi. Nobody had any doubt who had won. Certainly not Reddi. He promptly acknowledged his "debt" to the lady.

How had she brought it about? Partly, of course, it was the superior "mobilization" of votes by her, in other words the plane tickets, the money and the entertainments offered. But there were other factors. The sudden ganging up of the so-called "progressives" and the pro-CPI elements as a fighting force had upset the traditionalists in the party. Right from the beginning the Congress Party had been a convenient umbrella for all sorts of people and all shades of opinion, from one end of the political spectrum to the other. Part of the reason why Mrs Gandhi's leadership had been acceptable to all manner of people for so long was that she was immensely suited to lead a hold-all party. Unburdened by any strong convictions of her own, no "isms" ever mattered to her— except "self-ism." Whether it was capitalism or communism or socialism or scientific socialism, she was no more bothered about it than Sanjay Gandhi. Whether it was dollars or roubles or pounds or Deutsche marks, it was all the same to her, as long as they kept flowing in. But then perhaps that was what her non-alignment was all about.

The coming together of what some described as the "Ruski elements" threw the traditionalists in the party straight into the arms of Mrs Gandhi and Sanjay. They felt more comfortable there. Then there was the spectre of the Assembly elections. Still reeling under the impact of the March "earthquake" as *The Gaurdian* had called the Lok Sabha elections, the Congressmen were finding it hard to decide which way to go. Most of them had no doubt that if it came to elections, Mrs Gandhi was still the best bet. Many felt they would be safer with the "mother figure."

"If the results of the AICC have overtones of George Orwell's 1984," wrote S. Nihal Singh in *The Statesman*, "Congressmen have themselves to blame . . . Bansi Lal was punished and V.C. Shukla reprimanded, but in what can only be constructed as utter contempt of the electorate, the person responsible for all that had happened was confirmed as leader, and the party pretended that her son had simply vanished into thin air. To add a macabre touch to the proceedings, Mrs Gandhi chose the nominal Home Minister during Emergency to be her nominee for presidency. As a piece of effrontery, this Orwellian drama is unique in the annals of Indian politics."

Just a month earlier Mrs Gandhi had announced she was "out of politics."[19] She had of course added the clever rider, "just now". But there had not been one day, including the day that statement was made, when she was not immersed in politics. Now she was openly in it. Brahmanand Reddi had dutifully put her on the Congress Working Committee and the party's central election board. A good number of her supporters had been carefully inducted to the 21-member Congress Working Committee—Pandit Kamlapati Tripathi, Virendra Verma, Khurshid Alam Khan, V.P. Raju. Although Swaran Singh was there, Dev Kant Barooah was out. "Why wasn't Barooah included ?" reporters had asked Reddi after he announced his Congress Working Committee. All he said was: "He is not there in the list."[20] This led to doubts whether Reddi had even been consulted in the formation of his Working Committee! The AICC, too, had elected quite a few Indira followers: A.P. Sharma, V.P. Naik, C.M. Stephen, V.P. Narasimha Rao, S.D. Sharma and Mrs M. Chandrashekhar. But with them had come irritants like Chandrajeet Yadav and Das Munshi. They could be neutralized, but as Mrs Gandhi would soon find out she was still nowhere near having the kind of captive party that she wanted.

In spite of her successes in the party, she was still a "frightened"[21] person. Every day she was facing problems she had never known before. On 19 May the Janata Cabinet had decided to appoint a one-man commission to inquire into the "excesses" of the Emergency, her son's factory had been raided by the CBI and commissions of inquiry were being set up against him and Bansi Lal. Her sworn enemies in the Janata Government like George Fernandes were clamouring for her head, calling her all sorts of unprintable names. Even Charan Singh, the Home

[19] *The Statesman*, 7 April 1977.
[20] *Indian Express*, 13 May 1977.
[21] The word was used repeatedly by B.P. Maurya and other supporters of Mrs Gandhi to describe her state of mind at that time.

Minister, who until a week before she announced the elections in January 1977 had been supplicating to her for peace, was now threatening a Nuremburg-type trial for her. Her telephones, she was certain, were tapped, and she and her family shadowed wherever they went. Even the process of moving out of the house she had lived in ever since she left the Teen Murti House had been a "wrench" that showed on her face.

I had watched her from a distance the evening she moved to 12 Willingdon Crescent. For what seemed like hours she had stood alone on the verandah, leaning against one of the tall pillars, her eyes fixed on nothing in particular. What were her thoughts, I had wondered. Was she trying to pick up the threads of her life? Or was she contemplating the misfortunes of the immediate past and the eclipse of the present?

I had returned to the house about a week later, and this time I had gone in to talk to R.K. Dhawan. Marquees had gone up in the compound, Swiss cottages were being erected. Brahmanand Reddi, the newly elected party chief and half a dozen Congressmen arrived and waited to be called in. Slowly but steadily the show was beginning again.

Less than a month later, Mrs Gandhi was telling the TV interviewer David Frost that she had not been doing anything political at all, that she had felt a surge of relief when she got the news of her defeat "as if a tremendous rock had been lifted from my shoulders."

"Relief?" Frost asked in dismay.

"Relief. Utter, utter relief," she said.

Within an hour the interview had brought out all the insecurity, dissimulation, confusion and paranoia that had become such an inseparable part of Mrs Gandhi's psyche.

DF: What can you do now? Are you free to do anything? Are you free to travel?

IG: Well they haven't said anything openly, but I doubt if they would allow me out.

DF: But do you expect that to continue? I mean, someone said that the thing that really unifies the present Government, they're such a diverse group, is in fact, their opposition to, their detesting of, you, in fact.

IG: Well, I don't really know. But that they dislike me and

they think I'm a threat to them, so I'm told. Why I should be, I don't know. I am staying very quiet and not doing anything political at all.

DF: Were you ill served by the people around you?

IG: That some people kept the facts is evident from what happened subsequently. That is why they were the first people to be employed by the new Government.

DF: Which people ?

IG: Intelligence people and so on.

DF: You say intelligence people kept facts from you?

IG: Well, I don't—I mean, I think—I mean, I imagine that they did, because of this, that they turned out to be very close to certain people in the Opposition.

DF: Were there arguments—your son, I think, didn't want there to be an election ?

IG: My son had nothing to do with policy or decision making, nor did I discuss the elections or any other matter with him.

DF: But everybody says and many report of this, that your son was—that Sanjay took part in daily meetings of her emergency council, operated from her offices, and at times gave orders to Cabinet Ministers.

IG: There was no such thing as daily emergency meetings. And he certainly didn't attend a single meeting. Ever.

DF: He didn't. What about operating from your offices?

IG: Well, how can he? My offices are quite in a different block and he has never—I don't think he ever has seen my office.

DF: Never saw your office?

IG: I mean he may have gone there when I first became Prime Minister, I don't remember, but he certainly didn't during the Emergency.

DF: Giving orders to Cabinet Ministers and top civil servants?

IG: No, how can you? I mean this is absolutely ridiculous.

DF: But don't you think that his business activities were helped by being your son?

IG: Well, that may have been, but not because I said so, or somebody said so.

DF : Did you nearly destroy democracy?

IG : No, certainly not....

Watching her TV performance in England, writer Nirad C. Chaudhuri was amazed that she was not showing "even apparent harmlessness." He had thought the elections would have chastened her.... "Any woman or man with any moral sensibility would not have thought of remaining in politics after such a defeat as was hers. But she has no moral sense, she is egoistic, and besides obstinately courageous, and by virtue of these traits dangerous."

Almost prophetically, Chaudhuri had added: "That she would accept her exit from politics finally is inconceivable, and she is plainly showing signs of having recovered her courage and ambition...."

II

OUT AGAIN

But for her famous face, she could have been just another passenger taking an early morning flight out of Palam. She had come alone a little before six in an Ambassador. No pilot, no escort. Tense and awkward, she had entered the departure lounge, followed by a couple of aides who had come well in advance. She walked ahead of them, as though she needed nobody's help. Already a dozen or more passengers stood in queue at the Nagpur counter of the Indian Airlines. Alongside were other queues, for other flights. Before anybody could notice, she was at the end of the Nagpur queue, ticket in hand. Some curious passengers whispered to one another, some came out of their queues, some went on indifferently. Mrs Gandhi was trying so hard to act like a commoner.

Only for a moment, however, was she allowed to be in the queue. One of her aides took the ticket from her, and she moved away, a little reluctantly. For a while she stood in the centre of the hall, amid parallel queues and a knot of people gathered around her. A woman journalist-photographer from a Delhi magazine clicked away at her camera. Mrs Gandhi gave her a taut smile. She had not missed her morning facials, but dark pouches showed below her eyes, it seemed from lack of sleep or much crying. She wore a white sari with a plain border, a garland of beads round her neck—dressed already for the Ashram she was going to.

Four months after her fall, Mrs Gandhi was taking her first trip out of Delhi. It had been a tough decision. A few months ago she seemed convinced that the people of India adored and worshiped her, but no more. That confidence had been shattered. She was afraid of them, frightened what they would do to her. One day in late March, B.P. Maurya had suggested that she should go to Aligarh on 13 April to address an Ambedkar Jayanti meeting. Mrs Gandhi was taken aback. "Have you gone mad?" she had asked Maurya.[1] "Who will come to listen to me?" Y.B. Chavan and other senior leaders had felt that she should not go to the people. Even her supporters like Vasant Sathe thought she should lie low for some months and she herself had talked about retiring to Dehra Dun or some quiet retreat in the hills.

But Maurya thought differently. Resistance there would be, he was sure, but then it must be faced sometime. Why not now? Many people had sympathy for Mrs Gandhi, especially after her defeat in Rae Bareli. If there was any leader in the Congress who could win the people back to their side eventually it was Indira Gandhi, the only one with charisma. It was this more than anything else which made Maurya, Sathe and others stick to her leadership. "You must go out to the people," Maurya kept telling Mrs Gandhi. "You'll see they still want you." But she was not convinced. She thought he was just being nice.

One day there was a wedding in the house of a minor Congressman in one of the Trans-Yamuna residential colonies. Maurya pressed Mrs Gandhi to go to the wedding, as this would provide an opportunity, however slight, to judge the reaction of the people towards her. She was hesitant. "What's the use, Mauryaji?" she said. "Why create trouble at a wedding?" But Maurya was insistent. At last she gave in, on condition that no announcement would be made about her going to the marriage. "We did not tell anybody," recalled Maurya, "but no sooner had she arrived than word spread around and hundreds of people came out from the neighbourhood to have a glimpse of Mrs Gandhi." Later, he told her, "Madam, did you see how the people came rushing to see you?" But Mrs Gandhi, still sceptical, said: "You shouldn't take all this seriously. After all, people do gather at every wedding."

Left to herself, Mrs Gandhi would perhaps have taken a little

[1] B.P. Maurya in an interview with the author.

longer to come out of her cell. But the growing attacks on her family and herself would not leave her in peace. Sanjay and his wife had been harassed by officials at the Palam air-port and in Bombay a nasty crowd had surrounded the flat where they stayed. While some of the Janata leaders were hurling abuse at her day in and day out, her own party leaders were out to humiliate her. She was convinced of this when they made it obvious that she was not wanted in the Assembly elections in June. While Kamlapati Tripathi announced that she would campaign for the party candidates, the General Secretary K.C. Pant had declared that this was not true. "She will not campaign," he told reporters categorically. When asked if she would issue an appeal to the electorate, Pant had brushed the question aside with an indifferent "I don't know."

But to top it all, there was the *volte face* by Brahmanand Reddi himself. The "ungrateful wretch" that he was, Reddi was trying to show to the world that he was no "rubberstamp" President. No, the party manifesto had not been cleared by Mrs Gandhi, he declared at a Press conference. They had not even shown its text to her, he said. Soon after his election as the party President, the anti-Indira faction (that is what the great national leader, Mrs Gandhi, had been reduced to: a more faction leader) had started working on Reddi and had succeeded in weaning him away from her.

The final break between Mrs Gandhi and Brahmanand Reddi came over the candidature of Sanjeeva Reddy for the Presidentship. Reddi knew very well that Mrs Gandhi would tolerate anybody except Sanjeeva Reddy as the President. It was over his candidature that she had split the party in 1969, giving it a veneer of great radicalism. To have the same man in Rashtrapati Bhawan in spite of her was more than she could take. And yet, Brahmanand Reddi had gone along merrily with the other Congress leaders and announced the party's approval of Sanjeeva Reddy's name. There could not be a greater affront to Mrs Gandhi.

Peeved by all this, she was desperately looking for some support before she was strong enough to strike back. But where and how ? It was around this time that the Home Minister, Charan Singh, came out with yet another charge against her. On 13 July, he told the Lok Sabha that there was a thinking (*vichar*) on the part of the previous Government to shoot the political leaders in detention. "This was too much to take," recalled Vasant Sathe. "Some of us immediately went to Mrs Gandhi and told her she could no longer keep quiet, she must contradict the statement. And after she had done this, we suggested that she should begin going out to the people. We have to live or die with the people."

She herself was now keen to make a move, and surely she did not want to be in Delhi the day Sanjeeva Reddy was sworn in as President. If she was there and did not come it would be thought impolite. Better that she was away. But where? There had been invitations from Rae Bareli where people were already cursing Raj Narain, but that was certainly not the right place to begin.

"Why not go to Paunar?" suggested Nirmala Deshpande, a long-time disciple of Vinoba Bhave who had come over as secretary to Mrs Gandhi after her defeat. Mrs Gandhi immediately responded. The others too thought it was the best place to start from. For one thing it was away from the "Waterloo area" and for another it was in Maharashtra, still a Congress-ruled State. And so Paunar it would be.

Vinoba Bhave had long since been something of a *Sarkari Sadhu*; he had made the right motions, the right remarks in relation to Mrs Gandhi and had allowed the Sarvodaya movement to split vertically rather than let it go the way chosen by Jayaprakash Narayan. In a way he had even blessed the Emergency by raising his slogan of *Anusashan Parva*. And yet he and his ashramites had not been trusted fully; the Maharashtra Government had even raided the Ashram during the Emergency. Vinoba had called an all-India Acharya conference at Paunar to examine the various aspects of the Emergency, and the consensus that emerged had by no means been flattering to Mrs Gandhi:

> The detention of a large number of social and political workers, curtailment of civil liberties and press censorship were not good for the health of the nation if continued indefinitely...A fresh start is essential so that the Emergency can be ended.

Vinoba had reasons to be unhappy. Riding a high horse, Mrs Gandhi had not only ignored the recommendations of the Acharyas but even refused to meet Bhave's emissary, Shriman Narayan. But flung to the earth, Mrs Gandhi now needed not only Vinoba's blessings but also his good offices to lighten the pressure from the Janata Government.

But advice was all she got from her Sadhu during the half-a-dozen rounds of closed-door talks spread over three days. *Chalte Raho*, he mumbled to her repeatedly. Vinoba was observing *"karma mukti"* and would not talk about anything except "health and spirituality." What had he meant by the advice? One ashramite explained that it was only Vinoba's "advice for keeping fit—the more you walk, the fitter you are." But strangely, the advice was in line with the slogans raised by Mrs Gandhi's cheer-leaders at Nagpur and all the way to Paunar: *"Indira Gandhi aage badho, ham tumhare saath hain* (Indira Gandhi, move ahead, we are with you)."

It was like tonic to her. Briskly she travelled from Nagpur to Paunar that afternoon of 24 July, speaking briefly to crowds gathered by the roadside. The dark pouches under her eyes were gone. Every time she stopped to meet a crowd she looked brighter, fresher. Slowly but surely she was getting that old touch. I had seen tears in her eyes when a leader told her at Nagpur: "People are eager to listen to you." That did the magic. Later, when some people asked her when she would "come out," she said: "Haven't I already come out?" Emboldened by the adulation and the feet-touching that had gone on for three days at Paunar, Mrs Gandhi told a correspondent on her way back that there was really no question of her returning to politics, as she had "never left politics."

Back from Paunar, Mrs Gandhi sensed an entirely new mood overcome her party. Members were becoming stridently vocal and the fire was more and more directed on her. The first attack came at the Congress Parliamentary Party meeting on 28 July. The top leaders of the party, Reddy, Chavan, and even Tripathi, sat impassively as members from various parts of the country, particularly Assam ar d West Bengal, lambasted her for the destruction of "inner-party democracy" (a phrase so often heard in post-Stalin Russia) and "dilution" of the party's economic programme. The feeble attempts of some of her supporters to speak in her praise were drowned by the vehemence of the critics. F.H. Mohsin, a Lok Sabha member from Karnataka, and Mrs Purabi Mukherjee were still praising Mrs Gandhi, but had turned against the caucus. Kali Mukherjee, a Rajya Sabha member from West Bengal, who had recently demanded her resignation from the party, asked: "What is wrong in going to the press? Either she guides us in the right

way or she retires." Another Rajya Sabha member from Assam,
N. R. Choudhuri thought it was time "we make it clear to the
people that this is not the party responsible for the Emergency."

The attacks went on at next day's meeting of the CPP. "We will
never allow ourselves to be subjected to one person's rule," shouted
one member. Everybody was clamouring for "collective leadership
capable of independent thinking." A young fire-brand from West
Bengal, Saugata Roy, regretted that in her Frost interview Mrs
Gandhi had defended both the Emergency and Sanjay Gandhi. "But
Mrs Gandhi was not properly quoted in that interview," interjected
Sathe. He did not realize that there was no question of Mrs Gandhi
not being "properly quoted"—for it was Mrs Gandhi herself speaking on the TV; she was not being quoted. Sathe, it was clear, was
merely echoing Mrs Gandhi.

At a meeting with Pressmen at Paunar, she had said that the BBC
had given her an "undertaking not to do a thing like that." I had
decided to stay mum through it all, but this was too great a puzzle
to let go like that. Surely it deserved a clarification. "Sorry, Madam."
I ventured, "could you please elaborate upon that a little ?"

She threw me a sidelong glare before answering brusquely: "They
had assured me, they had given the undertaking."

This was as puzzling as the statement that I had sought to
clarify.

"What sort of undertaking, Madam?"

"Not to do that sort of thing," was her answer.

Still baffled, I asked : "Sorry, I still don't understand. What sort
of thing? Did the programme distort what you said? Were you
misrepresented?"

She was in a bind. Tapes had their advantages as well as their
disadvantages, a lesson that Nixon had learnt so well. Fumbling
for words, she repeated: "No, no they had given me a very clear
undertaking."

Knowing none of Frost's art, and having a pack of outraged
senior brothers of the profession ready to hound me out of the august
presence, I decided that discretion was the better part of valour.
I gave up, but could not understand where Frost had tripped. Was
it the way the BBC had presented the programme? It had started
with a huge caricature of a wicked, old and grim-looking Indira
Gandhi holding in one hand a smiling puppet in her own image.
And before the fade-out there were again the two caricatures of the

two Indiras. Nasty, but could these visual frills have struck if Frost had come up with another of those stale wishy-washy question-answer pieces which crowd our journals nowadays?

Mrs Gandhi now switched to dinner diplomacy. The cat, wrote Nikhil Chakravarthy,[2] was on the prowl—out to gobble up as much of the Congress as possible. The dinner was organised by Mrs Gandhi's friends from Karnataka and Devraj Urs flew down from Bangalore. As he waited for the guests to arrive that evening (4 August), Urs had ruminated over the mother-son syndrome. "After all she is a mother," he observed, pulling at his pipe. "She has realised her mistakes in politics."[3] What about the son? a correspondent had asked, and Urs had replied ponderously: "I think he should concentrate on mechanics, rather mechanical things. He is good at it. Politics? Definitely not. I had told him earlier, "Young man, you cannot do politics, leave it to your mother." This was a prelude to coming events.

The dinner diplomacy did not work. Mrs Gandhi had arrived, Kamlapati in toe. But neither Reddi nor Chavan turned up. Even the two deputy leaders of the CPP did not come. Much as the organisers tried to inflate the figure of MPs and former MPs who attended, everybody knew it was a poor show.

Besides, the others could play the same game. Next evening, about a hundred MPs turned up at the residence of a former Minister of State, V. A. Syeid Muhammad. There they deplored the "pernicious trend of dinner get-together in the cause of Mrs Gandhi"[4] and declared that "collective leadership does not mean a collection of three or four...it means revitalization of all the committees from village level to Parliamentary Board." Nothing could be farther from Mrs Gandhi's mind. A party not geared to her personal ends was no party to her.

She knew she would have to adopt other means of bringing the party down to her feet. She must revive her charisma with the people, she must show these defiant men that she alone mattered in the Congress. And all she needed now was the right opportunity.

The cannibalistic outrage at Belchi had hit the headlines some

[2]*Mainstream*, 30 July 1977.
[3]*The Hindustan Times*, 4 August 1977.
[4]*The Statesman*, 5 August 1977.

time back. In that remote village on the crime-infested border of Patna and Nalanda, a gang led by newly-rich Kurmis had gunned down 11 Harijans and tossed their bodies into a mass pyre. Here was a godsend for any leader wanting to project himself—or her-self—as the saviour of the poor. The opportunity was too good to miss. But Mrs Gandhi was hesitant. Belchi was not Nagpur or Pau-nar. It was in Bihar, the base of the JP movement, where the first shot against her was fired. Surely there could be trouble there. But her Bihar cronies, Kesari, Mishra and others were pressing her to go. It was not the same Bihar any more, they told her. Jayaprakash lay sick and frustrated in his Kadamkuan residence, his "youth power" gone, his dreams shattered. People were getting disgusted with the new rulers; even the Chhatra Sangharsha Samiti, or what remained of it, was talking of renewing their "revolution." Bihar had turned full circle. "It is waiting for you," Kesari told Mrs Gandhi.

She dilly-dallied for nine full days before taking the decision. Yes, she would go. Y.B. Chavan had set a date for visiting Belchi and she would beat him to it.

She preferred the front window seat in a plane, and usually got it. But this was small concession for a former Prime Minister and was only natural. In the first few rows sat her new cheer-leaders, excited and overwhelmed by the chance to be so close to her. The woman who couldn't spare them a minute till the other day now seemed to cling to any member of Parliament. It didn't matter if he was a de-fetaed one, for wasn't she one herself?

In the seat next to her sat Mrs Pratibha Singh, who was put in the Rajya Sabha for the good reason that her father, Sir C.P.N. Singh had been as loyal to Jawaharlal Nehru as he was to the Britishers. Another woman in the party was Miss Saroj Kharpade who had been important in making Mrs Gandhi's visit to Paunar a success. Being a Harijan MP, she was important to Mrs Gandhi who was out to become the greatest Harijan leader in the country.

Difficult to understand, however, was the presence in her en-tourage of men who had thrived on feudalism all their lives. But they too claimed to be the "champions of the downtrodden" and talked endlessly of Marx and Engels. One was a well-known protege of the late Krishna Menon and later of P.N. Haksar, the man behind Mrs

Gandhi's rise to glory. And another was a former protege of the Bihar Syndicate bosses whom Mrs Gandhi had fought in 1969.

The hubbub and excitement in the plane was confined to the front rows. Among the Congress sycophants were businessmen who had once hovered round No. 1 Safdarjang Road and now paid court to some of the Janata leaders. Indeed, Congressmen were not alone in playing safe; they were joined by these businessmen who had more at stake. Behind the first few rows, however, the passengers not only looked indifferent, but some even passed snide remarks. "There goes the operation come-back," whispered a young executive to his companion. Another wondered if the front row had a copy of the newspaper which carried a report on Congress MPs wanting the ex-Prime Minister to account for the election funds!

It was 6.50 a.m., 13 August 1977. Time to take off. A long day lay ahead of her. She sat back, looking out of the window. The pouches under the eyes had returned. She wouldn't take any of the cold drinks or snacks offered by the air hostesses. A member of her group, Bhism Naryan Singh, went up with an apple, but she wouldn't have that either. "People have no idea of her great reserves of energy," remarked an admirer. All praise for the lady, who they believed was poised for a come-back. And when that happened, would their lives change! We and we alone stood by you when you were down and out, they would remind her. Could she then turn her eyes from them? How little they knew her!

At the Amausi airport (Lucknow), Mrs Gandhi was swallowed by the crowd, while a local correspondent drew me aside. He took me to the other side of the airport building to see the commandered trucks which had brought the crowd—ten trucks for about 400 people. Managing her "reception" was her former Home Minister, Uma Shankar Dixit, who had begun his career as a "Muneemji" in Motilal Nehru's household.

At Patna, it was raining. It was a big crowd. About a thousand people, mostly Congressmen or people curious to see what she looked like in defeat. A row of Seva Dal volunteers stood dutifully braving the rain. As the plane taxied to a halt, the State Congress leaders rushed with their garlands. They were all expecting her to get down from the front door, but for some reason it was the rear door that was opened, and she was among the last to come out. The passengers preceding her had to tear their way through the shrieking crowd. The sight cheered her. It was contrary to anything she had expected in JP's homeland. Even some of her vocal critics in the party were around, to see how the people responded to her now.

It was a long motorcade that followed Mrs Gandhi's car on her journey to Belchi. As they passed, people came rushing from all around and at places there were welcome arches and even bands playing filmy tunes. At one point the band was playing: *Jo shaheed huey hain unki zara yaad karo kurbani...* and one wondered who they meant—the victims of Belchi or the victims of the March elections?

Belchi should have been the first stop but for some reason the motorcade was diverted to Biharsharif, a district town just off the route. She stopped at the Inspection Bungalow, presumably for a wash, and then some of the Congress leaders began saying that there was no question of her going on to Belchi, the road was bad. Within minutes a crowd had gathered and there was a scramble to get into Mrs Gandhi's room. There was much shouting and clamouring —friendly people who would not miss their only chance to see the lady at such close range. Young boys climbed the trees and people came rushing from all sides. When she came out, some Congressmen raised slogans and the new Congress chief of Bihar, Kedar Pande, started a blustering speech. And then they were all persuading her to speak. She spoke briefly, when lunch was announced. "You are going to have a sumptuous lunch," a Congress leader told a reporter, "We have cooked hundreds of chicken!"

"No lunch, let's leave," said Mrs Gandhi firmly. "The route is very bad," mumbled Kedar Pande. "No cars can reach Belchi." Not to be deterred, Mrs Gandhi said: "We shall go walking, we shall go there even if it takes us all night."

The motorcade moved out through the lanes of Biharsharif, and when it stopped everybody was scampering out after her. It was the Bari Dargah which has a tomb of Hazrat Sheikh Sarfuddin Ahiya Maneri. She had been told that if one prays at this dargah one gets whatever one asks for. She prayed, her eyes closed.

Some miles out of the town, the road petered out into a muddy track. The "road" to Belchi had begun. Mrs Gandhi's jeep got stuck in the mud and a tractor was brought to pull it out. But even the tractor got stuck. "There ends the trip to Belchi," quipped a TV cameraman. But Mrs Gandhi was out of the jeep, walking through the mud, followed by her cheer-leaders. "She can't go very far like that," said a Congress leader, frightened by the prospect of walking all the way to Belchi. "They say you have to wade through waist-deep water," he said, and slunk back to be in the comfort of his car.

Mrs Gandhi was still marching on, her sari raised above her ankles. "Of course I can wade through water," she was telling her frightened companion, Pratibha Singh. It was getting tougher every minute, but a thoughtful Babu Saheb of the area had sent his elephant to carry the lady to Belchi. "But how will you climb the elephant?" Kedar Pande and others asked her anxiously. "Of course I will," she told them impatiently. "This is not the first time I have ridden an elephant." Next moment she was sitting pretty atop the animal, her legs outstretched. But Pratibha was all nerves as she climbed, virtually clinging to Mrs Gandhi from behind as the tusker heaved up. A delighted cameraman burst into "Long Live Indira Gandhi." And Indira Gandhi smiled back at him.

From where she got off the jeep, it was three and a half hours to Belchi. But she made it, purely by her grit and determination, and was hailed as the "saviour of the Harijans." Who could imagine a Y. B. Chavan or a Brahmanard Reddi or any of those leaders doing what she had done. Around midnight, on her way back from Belchi, Mrs Gandhi was delivering a speech at a roadside college.

When she went to meet Jayaprakash Narayan early next morning, nobody could tell what she had been through the night before. She looked fresher than ever. And her 50-minute teteatete with her recent enemy left her even brighter. In fact, neither of them had looked so bright and cheerful for a long time. The old man seemed overwhelmed as he came out to see her off. Many were the interpretations of his widely quoted blessings to her—"a bright future, brighter than the bright past she had had." Some said she had won him over, others thought it was a "tongue-in-cheek statement" and still others said the statement was just by the way.

Whatever the blessings meant, the visit had certainly helped revive some of Mrs Gandhi's illusions about her own invincibility, illusions about her being the "only leader of the people of India" the words of Kedar Pande at the Sadaquat Ashram, headquarters of the State Congress. "There can be no compromise on the 20-point programme," Pande had declared, and the assembled Congressmen had given him a big hand. Only some days before, both Y. B. Chavan and Brahmanand Reddy had been to Patna and the crowd at Sadaquat Ashram had been large, but nothing compared to the one for Mrs Gandhi. "She might once again emerge as the leader just because there is nobody else who can draw a crowd anywhere in India," commented one of her critics in the party.

When Mrs Gandhi herself came to the mike, there was no repentance in her words, no remorse at all for the course she had taken. She went on and on defending the Emergency and at a brief Press conference afterwards she even denied there was any caucus around her. It seemed she had not even heard that word.

Came a nasty blow the very next morning. In pre-dawn swoops in Delhi and Kanpur, the Central Bureau of Investigation (CBI) arrested P. C. Sethi, former Union Minister for Chemicals and Fertilisers, Yashpal Kapoor, R. K. Dhawan and his brother K.L. Dhawan. Also nabbed were four businessmen who had allegedly been in league with R.K. Dhawan. While Capt. Vasudeva was arrested in Kanpur, K.L. Shroff, K.L. Bhatia and Sudhir Sarin were rounded up in Delhi.

The blow was particularly nasty having come so soon after what appeared a tactical victory for Mrs Gandhi. What with the elephant ride to Belchi and the benediction showered on her by the patron saint of the Janata Government, she must have thought her comeback was only a matter of time. And then suddenly the pre-dawn swoop, and of all days they had chosen 15 August for it!

That she was not addressing the nation from the ramparts of the Red Fort for the first time in 12 years was bad enough. Worse, she could not even be present. Her very own mouthpiece, the *National Herald*, which brought out the story next morning said that the Janata Government had made sure the invitation card was delivered late to her. But it is doubtful that she would have enjoyed the ceremony in any case, with her famous favourites in police lock-up.

The first information report prepared by the CBI said a sum of nearly Rs 6 crore from the Congress Party funds had been illegally invested in commercial enterprises in which Kapoor, Dhawan, Sethi and their associates had interests. Some of these "commercial enterprises," owned by friends and relations of the accused, were no more than a table, a chair, a telephone in some tiny room, with a signboard outside.

In remanding Yashpal Kapoor to police custody, the Chief Metropolitan Magistrate Mohammad Shamim had observed: "I have gone through the letter addressed by Mr P. C. Sethi, accused, to the former Prime Minister wherein the name of Yashpal Kapoor finds place as one who looked after the work of *National Herald* and collected funds in connection therewith...."

Kapoor was, in fact, much more than that. An old Indira retainer, he had been managing big sums right since the days of the Congress split, if not earlier. He had been one of her most useful operators and apart from resigning his official post to be her election manager in 1971 had taken full charge of defending her case. He had done it with "such skill and bluff" that she lost it. In spite of this, she entrusted him with managing her election in the 1977 poll and this time he did it even better, so well indeed that she lost to a joker. But he still retained her trust, which showed his importance to her. Dhawan came from the same stock, but he had wormed his way into the Indira court more through the son, which gave him even greater importance than Kapoor. It was Dhawan who had pushed the Maruti files through the corridors of power.

A singular feature of the Emergency had been the rank corruption in high places. "With Emergency, this (money grabbing) became one of the major preoccupations of the Indira kitchen, for which the entire entourage was mobilised, from Bansi Lal to Brahmachari, apart from the domestic hand like Yashpal Kapoor and Dhawan. And there were extra hands like Raghuramaiah. Presiding over this thieves' kitchen was Indira Gandhi, flanked by her heir-apparent, Sanjay."[5]

Reporters and cameramen had rushed early that morning to the residence of the Chief Metropolitan Magistrate, but the prize catches had left. They thought they would make up for it when one of Kapoor's sons began giving them an "eye-witness report" at the Tees Hazari court. He had only started, however, when a man came up and told him to "shut up." Present in the court, too, was Arjan Das, whose puncture repair shop had become a rendezvous of the "rulers" during the Emergency. He certainly looked down, if not out. But the others affected a brave front, with one of the accused, Sudhir Sarin, son-in-law of Yashpal Kapoor, giving "thumbs up" sign to the photographers. They were there to give R. K. Dhawan a "hero's ovation" when he got out on bail. Dhawan looked ashen, but his friends bucked him up with slogans of "R. K. Dhawan *zindabad*." If Kapoor and Dhawan were arrested, could Mrs Gandhi and Sanjay be far behind? Home Minister Charan Singh was already hinting darkly that much bigger persons would soon be

[5]N.C. in *Mainstream*, 20 August 1977.

arrested. "The net is getting closer and closer."[6] Though Mrs Gandhi managed a bold front, often defying the Janata Government to arrest her, her morale had once again dipped.

It was in one of her low moods that Maurya had suggested: "Why not take a trip to Hardwar? Don't you have some Mataji there?" Ah yes, Ma Anandamayee! Why not then go to her? That surely would give her new strength, but then there was a catch to it. To go to Hardwar she would have to pass the Charan Singh territory —Ghaziabad, Meerut, Muzaffarnagar, the very heart of Jat territory. Would it be safe? "Don't you worry about that," Maurya assured her. "After all, I too belong to that area. I shall make all necessary arrangements."

"I put all my energy, my entire cadre to organising the trip," recalled Maurya. "Since Mrs Gandhi was feeling insecure, I put my wife, daughter and small son in one car with her, along with a strong security man. In my own style, I manged two trucks and packed them with strong young men with revolvers and guns—all licenced, mind you. I placed the trucks behind her car and I myself was piloting in a Fiat. The first attack came in Shahadra, some stones and lathis. There was good fight. At Ghaziabad again our cars were attacked but the boys in the trucks managed everything. There was a huge crowd at Modinagar and again at Meerut. We were almost floating on the crowds. Then a big attack came at Muzaffarnagar. People threw shoes and chappals at her car and a dais which had been built was demolished. A big fight was going on, but still she spoke. By the time we reached Hardwar we were five hours late. She addressed a big public meeting. At night she went to address the workers of the Bharat Heavy Electricals, but there was organised resistance there, black flag demonstrations and much shouting. They were not allowing her to speak, but I told her to go on, my boys would tackle the mischief-makers."

Late in the night when Maurya went to leave Mrs Gandhi at the Anandamayee Ashram where she was to stay, she told him: "*Mauryaji, aap theek kahte the, bilkul theek kahte the Log saath denge*...(Mauryaji, you were right, absolutely right. People will support us)."

Anandamayee gave her a new garland of beads. She wore it and felt a new strength surge through her.

[6]Quoted in *The Hindustan Times*, 30 August 1977.

III

· THE FARCICAL ARREST

Sanjay Gandhi and his wife, Maneka, were setting up the badminton net in the garden. Rajiv's children, Rahul and Priyanka, played around. Mrs Gandhi was inside, talking to her lawyers, 'perhaps finalizing her strategy towards the Shah Commission. Suddenly, a functionary of the house came panting. "The CBI is here." There was nothing new in it, they had come before. "What do they want?" Sanjay had asked. The man was in a panic, the police officer wouldn't tell him anything except that he wanted to see Mrs Gandhi. Someone went to inform Mrs Gandhi, but she waived him away: "Tell them to wait." By then around 200 policemen were at the gate, about ten of them officers. It was 5 p.m. on 3 October 1977.

A friend who had come to see the family was stopped from entering. Sanjay leapt at the police, demanding: "What do you mean? This is not your property, show me your authorization to stop people." He had warrants, said the officer. Maneka rushed to the telephone and began dialling numbers. First P.C. Sethi, a former Minister of Mrs Gandhi and Treasurer of the Congress Party. She told him what had happened, but Sethi said he was unable to come. He too was under arrest and could come only after getting the bail. Then Maneka was dialling the newspaper offices, and when she didn't get some of the numbers she decided she would ring up her boys in the *Surya* office and tell them to pass the word around.

Then Rajiv took the phone, but N.K. Singh, the tall and handsome officer from the CBI, requested him not to inform anybody. He would like to keep the whole operation a secret. Singh had recently been to North and South America to gather evidence against the Gandhi family. He had returned only a few days earlier and been given this vital assignment.

A crowd had gathered, and still more kept pouring in. But Mrs Gandhi kept on with her meeting, apparently unruffled. This was no surprise to her. She had known it was coming. Indeed, she had repeatedly asked for it. In public speeches castigating the new Government, she had said defiantly: "They are afraid, they have no guts to arrest me." But in spite of her bold front, her fear had often come through. She didn't know what sort of a jail they would send her to, what it would be like. To a foreign correspondent who had wanted to know if she would be writing anything if put in jail, Mrs Gandhi had replied: "That depends on what they make me do. If they put me on hard labour, then of course it will not be possible for me to do any writing...." Not very strange fears for a woman who had presided over the terrors and tortures of the Emergency.

When Mrs Gandhi came out into the hallway, N.K. Singh was there. "I have come to arrest and offer you bail immediately," he told her.

"On what charge?" she asked with a frown.

"I can't tell you that," said Singh.

"Show me the warrant," she demanded. "Where's the FIR?"

"It is not necessary for the CBI to serve a copy of the FIR or a warrant of arrest," said the officer.

"That's Charan Singh's new law," interjected Frank Anthony, Mrs Gandhi's counsel who had been with her inside.

"Where are your handcuffs?" shrieked Mrs Gandhi. "I won't budge unless I am handcuffed. Bring your *hathkari*." She was in form, in full command of the situation.

A sheet of paper, later described as the FIR, was handed over to her. She sat down in her balustrade, reading it aloud to A.N. Mulla, a former Congress MP and judge, and Frank Anthony, who stood by her side. Mrs Gandhi had been charged on two counts: the jeep case and the awarding of a contract to a French company for oil drilling work in the Bombay High. She was alleged to have given the contract for over 17 million dollars whereas

another company was ready to do it for only four million. The
second charge related to a company being coerced into giving jeeps
worth Rs 40 lakhs for her election campaign. Among those to
be arrested along with her were K.D. Malaviya. H.R. Gokhale,
P.C. Sethi, D.P. Chattopadhyaya, all ministerial colleagues of
Mrs Gandhi; two Secretaries to the Government of India, B.B.
Vohra and S.M. Aggarwal; and three industrialists, R.P. Goenka,
M.V. Arunachalam and Jeet Pal. Another name that figured in the
arrest list was that of K.K. Birla, the industrialist and newspaper-
magnate, who had flown abroad a few days earlier, after a secret
meeting with Home Minister Charan Singh.

Having read the so-called FIR, Mrs Gandhi disappeared into
her bedroom, leaving N.K. Singh all by himself in the corridor.
Sanjay Gandhi was busy handing out the cyclostyled statement of
Mrs Gandhi (obviously ready from before) to reporters and TV
newsmen from all the world over. By then there were about 2,000
people jostling around in the compound of 12 Willingdon Crescent,
spilling over to the roadside. Some reporters had cornered Y.
Rajpal, DIG (Range), for details of what was going on inside, but
he said he was there only to supervise the law and order situation.
It was the CBI which was making the arrest.

Inside, the two jurists of Mrs Gandhi thought they were already
in a court room, arguing her case. Said Anthony, contemptuously:
As if they don't use jeeps in an election campaign! The charge is
that some jeeps were provided by one Modi here and some Modi
there and got through pressurization of some government officers.
What's wrong in getting and using jeeps during elections?

The charge was questionable, argued the former judge Mulla,
even under the electoral law what to talk of criminal law.

The Home Minister had made a ringing statement: "The wrongs
she committed and the indignities heaped on the nation—the
Constitution perverted, the fundamental freedoms forfeited, the
press muzzled, the judiciary robbed of its independence—called for
a trial on a Nuremburg model." But these were not the "wrongs"
and "indignities" with which she was charged. Comparatively, the
charges were "picayune," commented one American newspaper.[1]
Mrs Gandhi's lawyers had chuckled.

Seeing N.K. Singh standing outside Mrs Gandhi's door, a

[1]*Detroit Free Press*, 10 October 1977.

reporter asked curiously, "What are you waiting for?" and Singh had shot back, "I am not waiting, I have been made to wait."

All the bigwigs of the Congress, even her greatest detractors, were jostling with the crowd outside. Brahmanand Reddi, Kamlapati Tripathi, K.C. Pant, Bansi Lal, Radha Raman, Yashpal Kapoor, Shankar Dayal Sharma, A.R. Antulay and all the others you could name. Only the other day some of these leaders were out to cut her down to size. They did not want to soil their hands with the "misdeeds" of Mrs Gandhi. But now the Congress Party had promptly rallied behind her and declared that her arrest "is politically motivated and displays a highly vindictive, revengeful attitude on the part of the Government." The CWC called upon the Congressmen to meet the challenge of the arrest of Mrs Gandhi by organizing "an effective protest" throughout the country. The change had not come about suddenly; there was a background to it. The sudden pre-dawn arrests of a large number of Congress leaders on 15 August and the initiation of cases against hundreds of business firms had caused a flutter in the dovecots of the party. Congressmen all over the country suddenly felt insecure. Many thought the "Charan net" would come round their necks too. In Bombay, Rajni Patel, who had replaced S.K. Patil as the city's "strongman," was now anxious to close the ranks in the party. Treasurer P.C. Sethi had been a frightened, harried man, now he was positively jittery. Even Dev Kant Barooah had started telling his friends that this was "not the time to fight her."[2] By a single action the process of polarization in the Congress had been halted —at least temporarily. The arrest of Mrs Gandhi and her other colleagues left the Congress leaders dazed and bewildered.

Mrs Gandhi kept popping in and out of her room, as though waiting for the proper time. In another room, her daughter-in-law, Sonia, and her secretary, Nirmala Deshpande, were hurriedly packing a suitcase for Mrs Gandhi, the only indication that she would go.

It was not until 6.45 p.m. that she came out of her room, and was surrounded by reporters. Bansi Lal had coached them earlier to ask her as many questions as possible so that her departure could be delayed. And she too obliged them by answering any question, big or small, sensible or otherwise. She wore a white sari

[2]D.R. Goel in an interview with the author.

with a green border and Ma Anandamayee's *rudrakshamala*.

She had looked glum when she came out of her room, but brightened when the camera lights flashed and newsmen flooded her with questions. She had not much to say, except that she was sad that the people in Gujarat would be waiting for her next day and she would not be able to keep her date with them. In her written statement she had already dubbed the arrest as "political vendetta" and urged her people not to "subdue their spirit and determination...my individual liberty may go temporarily but what you have to think about and be prepared for is to fight the very real threat to our country's self-reliance without which we cannot successfully combat poverty or maintain our freedom. . . ."

"Why aren't you accepting the bail on personal bond," a reporter asked, and she snapped back, "Why should I furnish a personal bond? The whole thing is illegal. . . ."

The hallway was so jammed that she could hardly move and she insisted on the way being cleared for her to go out. Tension was mounting. Word had gone round that the CBI officials had asked for women constables to lift her into the car if she refused to go on her own. In the portico, some of the Sanjay goons had climbed to the top of the car, raising slogans of "Charan Singh hai hai." A mustachiod tough lay right in front of the car determined not to let it move. Mrs Gandhi had finally reached the car, almost three hours after the first arrival of the police, and it was clear that she had been buying time, letting the crowd swell so that she could get the maximum out of her histrionics.

As she stepped into the car, rose petals fell around her and slogans of zindabad rent the air and made her glow. The *pahelwan* was shrieking and yelling in front of the car, beating his breast, refusing to move. So impressed was Mrs Gandhi with the young man's performance that she picked him for her personal bodyguard that day onwards.

Amid sheer bedlam the car finally moved out of the porch and all the rest jumped into other vehicles. The sons and daughters-in-law got into the famous Matador, and in spite of protests from the CBI officers not to follow them, the others soon caught up with Mrs Gandhi's car, heading in the general direction of Agra. The CBI car, followed by 16 other vehicles screeched to a halt at a railway crossing. The gates were down. It was the Delhi-Bombay main line, time around 9 p.m. Mrs Gandhi wanted to come out for some fresh air and was allowed to do so. Her lawyers had also come out and wanted to know where Mrs Gandhi was being taken. To a tourist bungalow at Badkhal lake, they were told. "But that's outside the Delhi territory," the lawyers protested.

This was her chance. She set down on a culvert, refusing to move. The dim moonlight enhanced the drama of it all. Her supporters raised slogans as the CBI officers tried to get her back to the car. She wouldn't move. A slight scuffle followed, and Mrs Gandhi was pushed around a bit. The officers promptly apologised, but she was unmoved. There was no choice left but to go back to the city, which they did. This time they went to the other end of Delhi, to Kingsway Camp. There in the officers' mess, Mrs Gandhi spent the night, sharing a room with her companion, Nirmala Deshpande.

Next morning, the Press conference in Shastri Bhawan was a bustling affair. TV men and reporters fought for space. Charan Singh was riding high. Triumph marked his every movement, every word. There were lots of irrelevant and relevant questions. One was particularly irking. What would Charan Singh do if the charges against Mrs Gandhi failed? Would he resign? Why should he resign? he demanded, for he knew nothing could go wrong. It was his finest hour. For months his cronies had pestered him to do something about the woman who had sent him to Tihar. "What is this Shah Commission?" one of his close supporters egged him on. "Isn't it your creation? And yet, it is getting all the credit. Have her arrested, and the country will be at your feet. You will be the nation's hero."

He had wanted to do it on 2 October, the birth anniversary of Gandhi. But Morarji held it. Not on that day, he had said. Morarji was resolute. With his magistrate's mind, he had perhaps sensed that the case was not perfect, not worth the risk. But the Jat mind was equally strong, perhaps stronger, as it proved in the end. Charan Singh assured Desai that he had built up a "foolproof" case against her. So cocksure was the Home Minister that he ignored even the Law Minister.

Tees Hazari was like a crowded theatre. Rumours were rife about Mrs Gandhi. Would she or would she not be brought before the court? Back at the Kingsway Camp that morning, Mrs Gandhi had about finished with the fruits which Rajiv had brought. She was so afraid of danger to her life that she had refused to eat or drink

anything offered to her in the officers' mess that night. She had
carried her own water jug and would have nothing else. Anxiously
she awaited the next move of the CBI. At Tees Hazari the crowds
swelled and waited in vain. Mrs Gandhi was produced before the
court at Parliament Street. The place was already like a battlefield.
A sea of people, division everywhere. Janata Party supporters
shouting death for Mrs Gandhi. "We have been ditched," bemoa-
ned Maneka. Everyone had thought she would go to Tees Hazari,
and most of the Sanjay crowd had gathered there. But now it was
10 a.m. and the scene had been shifted at the last moment.

There were thirty people inside the court room, lawyers and
pressmen mainly, and some from the CBI. An air of expectancy
had descended. Everyone waited for the lady to arrive. And then
suddenly when there was a rush everyone knew who it must be.
Fighting her way through the crowd, with the expression of a
martyr, she entered. It had not exactly been manhandling, but then
it had been bad, all that jostling and pushing through the crowd.
She was all right, she told a reporter. In the green sari she wore
she looked sprightly as a sparrow.

The legal drama inside had begun. A sinister note was added to
it with the bursting of teargas shells outside, some of the smoke
drifting in, causing Mrs Gandhi to dab her eyes with a wet kerchief.
At the magistrate's podium with some reporters stood Rajiv and
Sonia watching it all. "Hang Mrs Gandhi" came the cry from outside. The battlelines out there were drawn sharp and clear. And
all that Mrs Gandhi did was smile. Brickbats flew. It was 80
minutes almost, and Mrs Gandhi was still in the dock. The order
was being dictated by the Additional Chief Metropolitan Magistrate,
R. Dayal: ". . .It is obvious that the forwarding of the accused
under Section 167 is founded on the existence of grounds for
believing that the accusation or information is well founded. The
fact that no prayer has been made under Section 167 indicates that
even according to the CBI there are no grounds for believing that
the accusation is well-founded. Further, the fact that even the
source of accusation has not been collected till now further indicates that there is nothing to show the existence of such grounds.
Thus there being no reasonable grounds for detention of the accused,
Shrimati Indira Gandhi, she is released forthwith."

Her smile grew broad as she heard the verdict. Sanjay Gandhi
rushed out in excitement and was swallowed in a crowd of hostile

Janata workers, but he returned and found his mother receiving the compliments of her admirers. Frozen in rapturous disbelief she stood for ten long minutes which seemed like eternity. "Even mummy herself couldn't have written a better scenario," a jubilant Rajiv Gandhi had chirped to a foreign correspondent that evening.

Bleary-eyed and dishevelled, she returned to 12 Willingdon Crescent. It was like the return of a martyr. And all because of the bad, messy handling by the Janata rulers. Kamlapati was stretching his legs outside. It had been a long wait. Reddi bustled in, rushed and garlanded her. Sweets and cakes were passed around. Sherbet flowed. Maneka played the hostess to perfection. The Emergency Goebbels, Shukla, wore a big toothy smile. The euphoria caught on like an infection, even Reddi. He went up with a cake to Mrs Gandhi. "Not today," she said, "it is my *vrat* (fasting day)." And she went about telling journalists the story of a yogi and a young peasant girl for the thousandth time. A pleasant and diplomatic conclusion to a whole grisly affair.

A big crowd had gathered outside the gate. She had to see it. Rajiv held the ladder, Sanjay was atop the terrace, acting the part of ideal sons. Gingerly, Mrs Gandhi went up the ladder. For fifteen minutes, nearly, she sat on the parapet, watching and waving the crowd. She watched them for so long that she didn't see them, like they didn't see her drama and heroics. Only she could do such things.

Almost the whole of that morning, a young reporter from a Delhi magazine, Sunil Sethi, was at Mrs Gandhi's house, watching the people come and go. He saw Maneka coming out, and Rajiv walking the dogs. Mrs Amateshwar Anand, Sanjay's mother-in-law, had for some curious reason made herself in-charge of the whole place. Yunus shuttled in and out of the house, and Mark Tully of the BBC discreetly looked for an entrance. In Mrs Gandhi's Secretary's room lay piles of telegrams, some congratulating her, others sympathetic. The reporter went up to say hello to Maneka, herself a journalist of sorts, but she refused to talk to him. However, her mother was sweet. "No dear!" she cooed, "I can't say anything." An air of well-being surrounded the place, made its atmosphere.

Later, when Mrs Gandhi came down from the roof, reporters

tried to stop her for a few words, but she did not respond. It was only when she saw Mark Tully that a sign of recognition passed her face. It seemed to say yes, the appointment stands. And indeed she had agreed to give the BBC another interview that morning. It would be in the front sitting room, very bare, with just one old sofa and a portrait of Nehru by some famous artist on the mantlepiece. Mrs Gandhi sat on one end of the sofa, and Mark on the chair opposite. It took the TV crew about ten minutes to set up the lights. Mark tried to engage her in small conversation but failed. She just ignored him. She was looking hysterical, absolutely battered. It could have been the sheer exhaustion of the court room, the teargas shells, the night in the mess, or all of these. Her eyes twitched uncontrollably. Everything was ready for the take. The camera was whirring. She heard Mark say 'OK we are ready'. Incredible, the transformation that came over her. Throwing the *palla* on top of her head, she was once again her old bright self. The lines had disappeared. She took Mark's questions straight on. He wanted to know her programme, what she wanted to do and so on. There was nothing new in the platitudes she offered, and then Mark asked if she was back in politics. That did it. She burst forth: "I don't know where you journalists get these silly ideas. I mean a politician is a politician and I am a politician for always... There is no question of coming back. ...I never went out. ..." She was hard, tough, quick and aggressive. The lights went out. Thanking Mark briskly, she whisked straight past him as though he didn't exist. It had been a 15-minute show in all.

That afternoon, Mrs Gandhi had come out looking stunningly fresh in a pink and white sari. Outside, writer Uma Vasudev had turned up in her red Standard Herald and was virtually hounded out by an extremely hostile crowd amid much obscenity and invective. Dhirendra Brahmachari, Mrs Gandhi's very own Swami and Yoga Guru, had arrived in his flowing snow-white muslin, a big smile on his glowing face. Hanging around was writer-poet Dom Moraes with a great big bouquet of flowers, sweltering in the heat, taking in the scene, bemused. He had looked dreadfully miscast with his flowers which he deposited inside. "What are you doing here?" a reporter asked him. "What do you think of the whole situation?" and Dom had mumbled in his incoherent drawl: "Oh, but they have just proved that they're such utter fools!"

And so she did keep her date with Gujarat. Blessed by her Brahmachari, she had taken the evening flight to Bombay. There were large crowds at Santa Cruz. Her arrest had sent shock-waves all over the country. Congress workers had held angry demonstrations and thousands had courted arrest. What would her next move be? a reporter had asked Mrs Gandhi, and she had said: "There is no move for me. I am not playing a game of chess." And one wondered what if she did! Next day she was in Gujarat. At a public meeting in Bulsar, the home district of Morarji Desai, she declared that she was back in politics!

It appeared as though once again Mrs Gandhi was up to her old game of wooing the poor and betraying them in the same breath. It had been the same in 1969, and it did not promise to be any different now, thought a woman correspondent covering the Gujarat trip. She recalled how the big business and industry profited from the nationalised banks, which were said to be for the poor.

It was a long, gruelling tour, covering a thousand kilometres in South Gujarat where the poor Adivasis live. The day started invariably at 7.15 a.m. and lasted till near midnight. Her trip took her to the most god-forsaken areas, where she was hailed variously as a "saviour," "revolutionary," and a "Desh Sevika." The rest of the leaders were all "Bakwas."

It was all so heady that her response was perhaps more over-whelming than she meant it to be. She said she would use them (the people) as a weapon to fight the Janata Party and one saw the chink in the armour. It was a reflection of her own deep-seated insecurity, her urge for survival. She had used the poor as her cannon-fodder before, and she was going to do it again. She was again at her promises: "My Government opened the road to opportunity for the poor, the downtrodden, the minorities, Harijans and women and students, and now the Janata Party is reversing all this, they are taking a different path. . . ."

At one meeting in Gujarat, she declared, "If they had guts they could have jailed me as a political prisoner. But they have no guts." With this tactics, Mrs Gandhi was now seeking to make a virtue of her own acts in jailing political prisoners by the thousands, leaving them in jail for months.

Her farcical arrest and release had given Mrs Gandhi just the break she had been looking for.

Charan Singh's *faux pas* had virtually torpedoed the Shah Commission. Suddenly it had cast a shadow on its achievements. The blotch-up had shattered its very atmosphere. In just a few days of testimony the horrors of the Emergency had come out in all their lurid details. It had exposed the pathetic charade of the Emergency monsters, brought out their enormous pettiness and showed them up for what they were. P.S. Bhinder, the great police terror of the Emergency days had broken down; Kishan Chand, the former Lt.-Governor, had tried pathetically to lay all the blame on his secretary, Navin Chawla; the CBI Director, D. Sen, had pleaded that he had only acted at the behest of the Prime Minister's "household"...It went on and on, each appearance more shamefaced than the one before.

The testimonies and cross-examinations before Justice Shah had left Congressmen in utter discomfiture all over the country, till their guilt and complicity began to show. Strange revelations had been made. A mere phone call from R.K. Dhawan or even his P.A. was enough to bring Ministers and high officials to their knees. No rules, no regulations. All had broken down. What had come out through the Commission was the collapse of the System itself.

Justice Shah had been hurt when Mrs Gandhi was arrested without his knowledge. As the Law Minister, Shanti Bhushan later put it, Shah had "reacted" to the arrest. At one point he even decided to stop further proceedings. "I would like to rethink about the functioning of the Commission," he said. Shah had gone to the Prime Minister and offered to resign, but Desai had urged him to continue. "It would be the end of the Janata Government," he told Shah. He had stayed.

But the question now being asked all around was : "Will she come?" When asked to appear on 7 November, she had requested for suitable alternative dates, saying she would be away on a tour of Andhra Pradesh. Her newspaper, *National Herald*, remarked gleefully how both the Government and the Shah Commission had been taken unawares by the non-arrival of Mrs Gandhi.

The other date given to her was 12 November, but she failed to turn up like in the past. Instead, she sent in a 17-page statement saying she did not know what "useful purpose will be served by my participation in the proceedings. If it decides, however, to hold the inquiry in accordance with law and in the course thereof summons me as a witness, I shall abide by its directives." It was clear that she would also sit in judgment on what was legal and what was not.

Her two main objections against the Commission were that the procedure followed was not legally justifiable and that as Parliament had ratified the Emergency, Justice Shah had no business to look into it. It was hard to see Mrs Gandhi in the role of martyr to the cause of civil rights and democracy, the same person who didn't give a damn about rounding up her opponents wholesale and herding them into jails, about gagging free speech and censoring the press, about using Parliament like a rubber stamp to change, retroactively, a law that got in her way. Mrs Gandhi had almost abruptly developed a touching faith in the right procedures, commented Arun Shourie in *The Indian Express*. Suddenly she was bothered about the dignity of Parliament and inconsequential things like the fundamental rights guaranteed by the Constitution.

Shourie had exposed the hollowness of her two objections. First, under the Commission of Inquiry Act, the Shah Commission could adopt such procedures as it deemed fit. As for Parliament ratifying the Emergency, even Hitler's Enabling Act which gave him absolute powers had been approved by the Reichstag with an overwhelming majority. And the records show that Hitler followed the prescribed procedure much more closely than Mrs Gandhi could ever hope to do.

As Ram Jethmalani,[3] the jurist, pointed out, concealed away in parts of Mrs Gandhi's letter were the "respect and fear" of cross-examination. An important grievance against the Commission was that people made reckless statements without any fear of being cross-examined. In other words, she was accepting that cross-examination was essential to check falsehoods. And yet, in the very next breath, she was charging that there had been "gruelling and long-drawn cross-examination by the Hon'ble Commission itself."

It was after her election case in Allahabad High Court that she had become particularly allergic to cross-examinations. Giving a devastating reconstruction of Mrs Gandhi's testimony before Justice Jagmohan Lal Sinha, which thoroughly exposed her

[3]*The Indian Express*, 17 December 1978.

"half truths and lies," Shourie concluded, "No wonder then that Mrs Gandhi's counsel (in Shah Commission) spent so much energy on trying to keep her from having to testify as a witness, from being asked questions and from having to say things under oath."

Mrs Gandhi was aware of Shah's ruthless scrutiny and had seen others squirm under it, and all the time she was afraid that this might be her own fate.

She almost gave herself away, when, with rhetorical flourish she proclaimed that no government could function in fear of inquisitorial proceedings by a subsequent government.

What gave Mrs Gandhi a handle against the Commission was the endless bluster of Charan Singh, here, there, everywhere. He had proclaimed at a public meeting that "a warrant will be issued, if necessary, to bring Mrs Gandhi before the Shah Commission"[4] and again that "if the Shah Commission came to the conclusion that there was *prima facie* case against Mrs Gandhi, the Government would prosecute her."[5]

These were just the chinks Mrs Gandhi was waiting to pick on in order to gain time. Objecting to the first statement, she wrote to the Commission: "...Mr Charan Singh's statement underlines the fact that he looks upon this Hon'ble Commission as an adjunct of the Janata Party in general, and of the Ministry of Home Affairs in particular." As to the second statement, she stated, "The Home Minister has now made it clear that on the *ex parte* declaration of guilt, he will initiate prosecution."

The letters showed how her mind—more precisely the mind of her lawyers—was working. She would first refuse to testify under oath and later claim that the verdict of the Shah Commission was *ex parte*, that she was not given a chance even to state her version, which was just what one of the ardent supporters of the mother and the son sought to do in a TV discussion on the Maruti Report.[6]

For weeks Mrs Gandhi had held prolonged discussions with her legal advisers on the strategy she ought to adopt towards the Shah Commission. When she turned around for a sensible political advice on the matter, she found a vacuum: there was not one political mind worth the name around her. Whom could she ask?

[4]*The Indian Express*, 5 December 1977.
[5]*The Statesman*, 5 December 1977.
[6]Telecast by Delhi Doordarshan on 14 September 1979.

Her Sathes and Dhawans and Yashpal Kapoors?

In desperation, she sought the advice of P.N. Haksar, who had at one time been the architect of her power and glory. He was one man who had always told her in her face what he thought was right, without bothering for her reaction. He had refused to be a party to her weaknesses for her son, and had preferred to go out rather than demean himself to the level of a courtier. After what the Sanjay mafia had done to his family, no other man in his place would have even cared to give any advice to her. But Haksar was above such narrowness, and even had some lurking sympathy for Mrs Gandhi, for after all she was the daughter of Jawaharlal, a leader he admired.

Haksar's advice to Mrs Gandhi was to face the Commission boldly and say that the imposition of the Emergency was *her* decision as the Prime Minister. It was not right for her to avoid making a testimony before the Commission. As for all the statements that her former Ministers like Pai, Subramaniam and others had made, Haksar thought she should pity them rather than be angry. Mrs Gandhi must have realized it was no good asking Haksar. He functioned on a very different wavelength than hers. To follow his advice needed courage and moral fibre which she did not have. It was all right to make brave speeches about the Emergency, but to be cross-examined about it was something she could not stand up to.

Some of her lawyers did feel that if she agreed to make a statement under oath, it would entitle them to cross-examine the Ministers and officials who had given damaging statements against her, and it was possible that many of them could be demolished. That would certainly be an advantage. But on the other hand, the prospect of facing the gruelling cross-examination of Justice Shah was a chilling one. It was argued, much to the relief of Mrs Gandhi, that the former Chief Minister of Tamilnadu, Karunanidhi, had defied the Sarkaria Commission and had not suffered much for it. Her mind was made up.

When the Commission issued a formal summons, Mrs Gandhi had no choice but to go to the Patiala House.

9 a.m. on 9 January 1978, she arrived with her lawyer, Frank Anthony, son Rajiv and her two daughters-in-law. The very first words of Anthony made it clear that they had chosen to go in for a long legal battle against the Commission. As B.P. Maurya later

confided,[7] they had decided to adopt a delaying tactics. The
Janata Government, they were convinced, would eventually crack-
up. It was only a matter of time.

Frank Anthony told the Commission that his client was not
obliged to file a statement (Justice Shah had asked for her statements in connection with the 11 specific points that had been
earlier raised in hearings). He charged that the Commission was
politically motivated and that Justice Shah had overstepped his
powers.

Mrs Gandhi sat facing Shah, but somehow could never meet his
eye. Her face was a veritable mirror which reflected a range of
expressions from disgust to cynicism to amusement. Sometimes she
clutched her bag or fiddled with its contents. Once in a while she
would leaf through a government publication, her eyes vacant as
she looked around unseeing.

Among the witnesses present were Pai and Subramaniam. P.C.
Sethi sat biting his nails.

The drama climaxed on Wednesday, 11 January, when Justice
Shah asked Mrs Gandhi if she would make a statement under oath.
She had remained absolutely still and expressionless. Behind her
was her family, including Sanjay this time.

Justice Shah had repeated in his clear, stern voice: Mrs Gandhi,
will you make a statement under oath?

There was still no expression on her face. Anthony went up to
her and whispered something. Slowly she rose and went up to the
podium. In a trembling vo'.e she said: Sir, I decline to make a
statement under oath. I am legally not bound to make it. It
violates the oath of secrecy I have taken.

Justice Shah said: Will you make a statement or take the consequences ?

No response. Her defiance was complete.

Calm and unruffled, Justice Shah began dictating his order. She
was to be tried for having declined to give a statement before the
Commission. Mrs Gandhi had succeeded in dragging the Commission to her own level: a mere complainant in a local court.

Her refusal to testify before the Commission, said M.C. Chagla,
was for fear of exposure to "public condemnation and public
obloquy" in case the Emergency excesses were established. She had

7In an interview with the author.

sought to convert the Commission into a political platform. Describing her as a "living enigma," Chagla said it was difficult to understand how her mind worked. She never had any intentions to help the Commission find out the truth.

Mrs Gandhi feared nothing more than the truth.

IV

THE SECOND SPLIT

The second Congress split coincided with two important political events: President Carter's visit to Delhi and the sacking of Devaraj Urs. It wasn't a mere chance. While the imposition of President's rule in Karnataka was directly linked with the split, the synchronisation with Carter's visit was only another example of Mrs Gandhi's uncanny sense of timing and her great penchant for hogging the limelight. What with a jumbo jet carrying the world's top media personalities, including the famed Barbara Walters, arriving with the U.S. President, there couldn't have been a better time to show to the world that far from having faded into oblivion she was very much in the centre of things.

But the split also coincided with a third happening which went unnoticed, and yet had a direct connection with the Congress breaking up for a second time in eight years. It was the take-over of the *National Herald* by Yashpal Kapoor. On 31 December 1977, even as *pandals* were being set up for Mrs Gandhi's convention of Congressmen, Kapoor walked perkily into the Delhi office of Nehru's dying newspaper and announced that it would live. "*I* am going to run it," he told the *Herald* workers, much to their surprise. They had almost given it up for lost. The company had been in such utter straits since the fall of Mrs Gandhi that in November the then Managing Director, Mohammad Yunus, had sought Mrs Gandhi's permission to sell it off. The paper's sources of revenue, largely dubious, were drying off. Bansi Lal,

Narayan Dutt Tewari, Zail Singh, Jagannath Mishra and the other satraps who had kept it going through all sorts of patronage, official and otherwise, had been thrown on the dustheap. The hens that laid the golden eggs had all been slaughtered at one go. Now it was just not possible to keep the paper going, Mrs Gandhi had been told. In early December the board of directors formally decided to sell the company's land and assets. On 23 December, right in the middle of a political tea party that Mrs Gandhi had given at her home as part of her manoeuvres to capture the Congress, came the loud slogans from the gate: *"Nehru ke naam ko mitti me milane wale barbad hon, barbad hon* (Let those who are dragging Nehru's name into mud be destroyed)." It was a torchlight procession by the workers of the paper which had suddenly ceased publication.

This was as great a discomfiture for Mrs Gandhi as the poor attendance at the tea party. While she had expected at least a hundred MPs and former MPs to come, not half the number had turned up, the most important of them being her own pet cronies: Yashpal Kapoor, Vasant Sathe, Kalpnath Rai, Saroj Khaparde and others. She had meant the party to be a sounding board to ascertain how many would come for the convention she was planning. She felt frustrated, and to make it worse there was this crisis in her newspaper which she needed so much to build up her image. The two crises, the one in the party and the other in the newspaper, had moved towards a climax almost together. It seemed the lady's fluctuating morale curve had taken another dip.

Mrs Gandhi called Uma Shankar Dixit and told him to explore the possibility of keeping the paper alive. Dixit had managed the company for several years before he resigned to become her Minister. He thought it over and told Mrs Gandhi that he could keep the paper going only if she gave him Rs 25 lakhs. "Where can I get so much money?" Mrs Gandhi said. And so on 26 December the board of directors met again and decided to call an extraordinary meeting of the shareholders on 3 January to ratify the sale proposal. But instead of that happening, Yashpal Kapoor took over as the Managing Director of the Company on 4 January 1978, just two days after Mrs Gandhi's "real" Congress was floated.

It was no magic wand that had done the trick. What had saved the newspaper—at least temporarily—was hard cash that came from Karnataka, a part of the deal between Mrs Gandhi and

Devaraj Urs for splitting the Congress Party. Much as Mrs Gandhi
was struggling to get a captive party to help her and Sanjay out of
their personal predicament, she was not in all that rush to split
the party. Left to herself, she would have liked to wait until she
could grab the whole of it, which she thought was only a matter of
time. Her arrest and release had given her a tremendous boost and
she could see many a defiant Congressman weakening.

She could wait, but not Devaraj Urs. The dismissal from Chief
Ministership was for him the proverbial last straw on the camel's
back. The Central Congress leadership had already foisted his
political rival, K.H. Patil, over his head as the President of Karnataka Pradesh Congress Committee. It was the machinations of
Patil, helped by his patrons at the Centre, which had eroded
his strength in the legislature party and brought about his
fall. Almost overnight the edifice Devaraj Urs had built up so
diligently over the years seemed to be crumbling. He could clearly
see what would happen in the Assembly elections which were
round the corner. Between Brahmanand Reddi at the Centre and
K.H. Patil lording it over the State party organisation, they would
ensure that Urs' men were denied party tickets. Instead, the
Vokkaligas and the Lingayats, the two upper castes of Karnataka
which had shared political power for decades, would be back
again in all their glory. All the battles that Urs had fought against
the stranglehold of these castes would have gone in vain. He would
become the non-entity that he was before Mrs Gandhi picked him
up in 1969 to lead her new Congress. What was worse, he feared
he might even end up in jail. The Grover Commission of Inquiry
set up by the Janata Government had already indicted him on
several counts and rumours were rife that he might be arrested.
It was a low he could never have foreseen.

Nobody knew Urs' predicament better than Mrs Gandhi. He had
camped in Delhi for 21 days in December to persuade her that the
only option open for her was to break away from the Congress
and become the party president herself. She had to have her
own party to fight for her. The rest of the leaders were in any case
no good, all tired and exhausted men with no future. "Let's not
carry those millstones round our necks" was his refrain. At one
point, when Mrs Gandhi showed her reluctance, Urs assumed an
aggressive posture and began talking about the possibility of floating a new Congress party for South—the "South Indian Congress."

He had even started secret negotiations with M.G. Ramachandran, the actor-Chief Minister of Tamilnadu, A.K. Antony, Chief Minister of Kerala and Vengal Rao, Chief Minister of Andhra Pradesh, towards that end. Though it was still more of a pressure tactics, she was genuinely concerned. Urs was about the only political heavyweight on her side, the only one who could give some respectability to her political following, for while all the others were mere drummer boys floating in the void, Urs was the only one who had grown political roots of his own. What was more important, if Urs left she would lose one of her biggest sources of money.

It was Yashpal Kapoor who suggested to Mrs Gandhi that if she was going for a split in the party, she must make the "right use" of the opportunity. Urs' need for a split in the party was more urgent and so he would willingly agree to pay any price for it. She needed money to run her paper, didn't she? So why not "kill two birds with the same stone?" Kapoor told her. Kapoor himself was put on the job. In his own casual, nonchalant manner, Kapoor threw the hint to Devaraj Urs. If you are going to have a new party you must have a daily newspaper to build it up, he told Urs. A newspaper was already there, one with a great tradition. Unfortunately it had fallen on bad times. All that had to be done was to pump in some lakhs. That did not sound like a great problem to Urs. As a fund collector he was second only to a man who was dead and gone, Lalit Narayan Mishra. Raising a few lakhs of rupees for the *National Herald* would be no problem at all. It was only when Kapoor mentioned the amount required that Urs realized it was almost a blackmail! Seventyfive lakhs! That sounded rather steep, but Urs had played with big money, he was not going to give up on that account. After a few days of negotiations, a deal was finally struck: Mrs Gandhi would split the party the moment Urs delivered Rs 52 lakhs, which, Kapoor said, was "the minimum requirement" to get the *Herald* going.[1]

Initially, Mrs Gandhi announced 31 December and 1 January as the dates for her party convention. But till the very last moment she was not willing to show her cards. Her supporters kept on describing it as a "convention for unity." The hard-boiled operator that he was, Kapoor had insisted that Mrs Gandhi should not say

[1]The account is based on interviews with Congressmen and employees of the *National Herald*.

a word about declaring a new party until the cash was in hand. According to the schedule, the money was to arrive by 30 December, but for some reason it was delayed, and the convention too was put off by a day.

It was at 12.50 p.m. on 2 January that the convention chairman, Kamlapati Tripathi suddenly cut short the man who was delivering a speech at the moment and introduced a resolution unanimously electing Mrs Gandhi as President of the "real" Congress Party. Many thought that 12.50 p.m. was the time set by astrologers for splitting the party. But the reason was far more important, if mundane, than astral timing. What Tripathi had waited for was a "green signal" from Mrs Gandhi who was at 12 Willingdon Crescent, ostensibly for an interview by Barbara Walters. The sudden announcement was an indication that the precondition for the split had been met. The cash had arrived!

The split was the climax to an operation that had begun soon after Mrs Gandhi's triumphant trip to Gujarat. Her arrest and release had proved a high point in what had seemed to many as her inevitable drive back to power. But in spite of all her new martyr's halo and the morale boost she had got, Mrs Gandhi was a jittery, frightened woman. Charan Singh had started saying that she would be arrested again, that this time she would be booked for far more serious crimes. Mrs Gandhi herself told some of her close supporters that she would be rearrested on 12 October. For nearly a fortnight after her first arrest she lived in constant fear, except during the few days she was away in Gujarat. She hardly slept at night and at the slightest noise she would peer out of her doors.

It was a real drama that was enacted in the night of Monday, 10 October. Suddenly Mrs Gandhi raised an alarm, and everybody went rushing to her. It was almost midnight. Mrs Gandhi was certain the police had come to pick her up again. Some people ran out and sure enough there was a police van backing out near the gate. It turned out that the van had only come for the change of guards outside her house. Even so, Mrs Gandhi was so highly strung that everybody sat through the night in vigil. And after that day a band of muscular Youth Congress volunteers was put on round-the-clock duty.

Notices had begun arriving from the Shah Commission. Sanjay

was in a state of blue funk with cases being instituted against him all over. His great chum and hatchetman, Bansi Lal, had been handcuffed and paraded through the streets of Bhiwani, and already there were reports that R.K. Dhawan might turn an approver! "I'll get them, I'll get them all," he would often rave in the house. For some time he had even stopped joining the family at the dinner table, and when he did join he would hardly utter a word. "We do nothing except stare at the ceiling all evening," Maneka had confided to friends. Of course everything had brightened up after Mrs Gandhi's brief arrest, but the undercurrent of fear and anxiety was still very much there.

Mrs Gandhi knew there was not much time to lose. She must get a hold over the party. Perhaps if she became the president of the party, the Government would not dare to arrest her. In any case it would help to politicise her predicament and she would have the partymen acting as her Praetorian guards. She thought there was already a change in the behaviour of some of the defiant Congress leaders. They were showing greater deference towards her than they did before the Janata Government committed its blunder. Brahmanand Reddi had gone rushing to her house when he heard of her arrest and had garlanded her with great aplomb on her return from the court next day. Even at the organisational level, the party had lost no time in condemning her arrest. All these had given Mrs Gandhi and her supporters the impression that the party leaders were at last ready to capitulate.

But within a week or ten days they realized that the Congress leaders would not easily give up their newly-grown spines. Nothing less than a full-scale offensive would do. Some of the principal storm-troopers of Mrs Gandhi, including Vasant Sathe and Abdul Rehman Antulay, assembled at the Karnataka Bhawan in New Delhi one evening and passed a resolution saying that Mrs Gandhi should be elected the party president. They even thanked Brahmanand Reddi for having "agreed to step down in her favour." As Reddi clarified later, "I was only being respectful and considerate to her feelings and I had said that I am prepared to consider stepping down if [she asks me. But she never asks for anything herself. Never. She wants others to do everything for her."[2]

[2]*India Today*, 16-31 January 1978.

The resolution had only sharpened the resistance of the party managers opposed to her and they united behind Reddi. The Indira brigade gathered again at the Karnataka Bhawan, which had by then become their "base headquarters" and worked out a new strategy. They had chosen the one-day AICC session in Delhi on 15 October to launch a new offensive. Though the broadside was started by her cronies, it was the lady herself who turned up dramatically at midnight to deliver the major thrust of the attack. She accused the senior leaders on the dais for having sold their souls to the devil. They were all conspirators against her, she was telling them, and in what was clearly a resurgence of her old megalomania, she declared: "I am the country, I am the party, and even after my death my memory will continue to inspire the people to fight for my ideals." There were no tears now, only punches, hard-hitting punches. Gone was the time for humility.

As Reddi was showing no inclination to step down, Mrs Gandhi's men had started a signature campaign on a requisition notice calling for an AICC meeting to elect a new president. Soon they were claiming they had collected over 400 signatures. They wouldn't, however, reveal the names. And it was found that from the Congress Parliamentary Party nine of the 15 AICC members had not signed and yet the requisitionists were claiming their signatures.

Though others may not have known, the poker players themselves knew fairly well how the cards were stacked. Of the six Chief Ministers in the country at that time—A. K. Antony (Kerala), Vengal Rao (Andhra Pradesh), Vasant Rao Patil (Maharashtra), S.C. Sinha (Assam), Williamson Sangma (Meghalaya), and Devaraj Urs (Karnataka)—only Urs was fully committed to the requisition move. The others were either against it or hesitant. Even Vengal Rao, who had always been opposed to Brahmanand Reddi and had even threatened to resign when he was elected party president, had made up with him, and ironically it was Mrs Gandhi who had been responsible for the patch-up between them.

Mrs Gandhi and her supporters were now eager for some face-saving device. They drew up what they called their "nine-point charter of demands" stipulating, among other things, that Reddi must take all major decisions with the concurrence of Mrs Gandhi, that he must reconstitute the Parliamentary Board and

and the Working Committee in consultation with her, that he must suspend all disciplinary actions taken against members after the Lok Sabha elections. Acceptance of the "charter" would have virtually reduced Reddi to the position of a rubber stamp. He rejected it, and let it be known that the requisitionists could go ahead and do what they liked. Knowing that it was Mrs Gandhi who was on weaker grounds, he just sat back in his home, waiting for her to make the next move.

She took him unawares by her next move, arriving at his house well after midnight. For so long had she kept tabs on all her men that she knew even the personal habits and lifestyles of each of them. She knew midnight or after would be the best time to catch Reddi without his group around him. It was an unusual step on her part, but the times were unusual. She had received yet another notice from the Shah Commission to appear on 21 November and it was already 17 November. She had to stop more Congressmen from appearing before the Commission; enough damage had already been done.

If nothing else, the midnight visit brought about a thaw and led to fresh negotiations. Next day two drafts were prepared, one to be issued by her withdrawing the requisition and the other by Reddi calling for unity in the party. A tacit part of the understanding was that the Congress leadership would not insist on action against Urs who had defied their directive to drop one of his ministers for his anti-party utterances at Bangalore. And so ended a six-week old drama, but only to reopen soon.

It was at best a tactical retreat for Mrs Gandhi. She had gained nothing, except a meaningless call for unity by her former "doormat", Brahmanand Reddi. Obviously it was a defeat and she was not prepared to see herself a loser in the party which until recently was under her sway. She was full of impotent rage. Even her fears had grown, more so after her trip to the South in October-November. It had been all smooth until she was this side of the Tungabhadra, but the moment she had crossed to the other side, stones and brickbats flew in. The roughest was at Chikmagalur, which was to return her to Parliament just a year later. So rough and violent were the crowds that she had to hide herself behind riot shields to speak at meetings.

She returned from the trip shaken—"in fear of her life," recalled B. P. Maurya, one of her closest supporters at that time. "People will kill me," she told him, and brought out the threatening letters she had received. She was so frightened that Maurya and his wife started sleeping at Mrs Gandhi's house to give her a feeling of security. "This went on for nearly a month. We were almost living there." Maurya had seen the "mighty Durga" in her true self.

For her political ally, Devaraj Urs, the situation was no better. In spite of the so-called truce at the Centre, his foes in Karnataka were pulling no punches. They were out to do him in, and he could see his future was getting blighted. He was under attack from all sides. Since he was one of the main pillars of Mrs Gandhi's politics, the Janata Government seemed determined to finish him. Even the Governor, Govind Narain, was gunning for him; he would miss no opportunity to knock down a Chief Minister who had treated him like dirt.

Urs was getting desperate. He worked hard on Mrs Gandhi to convince her that unless she acted fast she would lose even her southern foothold. With the elections in Andhra Pradesh, Karnataka and Maharashtra only months away, it would be fatal to leave her enemies in control of the party. Unless she could choose her own candidates for the polls, she would be finished. He was virtually pushing Mrs Gandhi to take one of the two courses: either capture the party or split.

She was still for trying the first course. In what was virtually a plan for a Nazi putsch, her supporters backed by the Sanjay goons were to storm the CWC meeting scheduled for 5 December and force the leaders to go on bended knees to Mrs Gandhi and persuade her to join the meeting. And once this was done, the next step would be to declare her as the Supreme Leader of the party—there and then. But Mrs Gandhi grew cold feet at the last moment and the "coup" plan aborted.

She turned up at the meeting herself to try and block any further appearance of Congress leaders before the Shah Commission. Urs, Maurya, and A.P. Sharma put up a vigorous demand that the CWC should put a total ban on any Congressman appearing before the Commission. As a sop to Mrs Gandhi, it was decided that Congressmen would be "advised" to stay away from the Shah inquiry. Next day the CWC took up the Karnataka tangle, but it only ended in acrimonious exchanges. Mrs Gandhi's complaint that her followers were being "persecuted" by the Congress leadership brought the acid charge of Y.B. Chavan that she herself had been running the party in Uttar Pradesh as a "royal preserve."

That night Mrs Gandhi's "war council" met at 12 Willingdon Crescent and Urs launched an offensive against Chavan and Reddi. Next day, he rebuffed the Congress leadership openly by refusing to meet their emissaries, Y.B. Chavan and Tripathi, who was still playing the role of Narad.[3]

Mrs Gandhi finally gave in to the high-voltage pressure of Urs and wrote out a letter resigning from the CWC in protest against the "dangerous drift" in the party's internal affairs. Describing it as a "decisive moment" in her life, she charged that the party had been "rendered incapable of playing its legitimate role in national affairs."

But though she wrote the letter on 9 December she sat over it for full nine days. On 10 December she even attended a meeting of the CWC for three hours without showing what was on her mind. It was delivered to Reddi on 18 December, significantly by one of the lieutenants of Urs, F.M. Khan, who was soon to ditch his master to join the Sanjay brigade. The letter gone, Mrs Gandhi left on a pilgrimage to Vaishno Devi, presumably to seek the blessings of the goddess at this "decisive moment" in her life. But if she had thought that her resignation would throw the Congress leaders off their rocker and they would come pleading to her she was mistaken. They had developed a little more punk than she had thought. The party, said a senior member of the CWC, had gone out of its way every time to give all the protection she needed. "To say the least we have mortgaged our souls to her for 11 years—many of us who are much senior to her in the organisation."[4]

As Brahmanand Reddi said in a speech at Hyderabad later, "She wanted us to fight, take to the streets and go to jail. We are not afraid of going to jail. We have been to jail for years while she has been to jail only for nine months. . .But have we to involve ourselves in a scuffle with Janata leaders? Or should we agitate to support Sanjay Gandhi, Bansi Lal or Yashpal Kapoor?"

That was precisely what Mrs Gandhi had expected Reddi to do.

[3] A legendary figure of the Hindu mythology who acted as a messenger of gods.

[4] *The Statesman*, 20 December 1977.

Wasn't Reddi the man who had showered encomiums on Sanjay only a year ago? Mrs Gandhi and her supporters would often show the people what Reddi had said on Sanjay's birthday in December 1976 : "He represents the fourth generation of a remarkable family that has been at the forefront of Indian political scene and led the nation to freedom...*He has also an undoubted charisma of his own*...*In the short span of a few months, he has established himself as the most outstanding youth leader in the country. In the new atmosphere in the wake of Emergency, Sanjay is giving them (the youth) a sense of direction, participation and fulfilment.*" (Italics mine)

What surprise, then, if she had expected better from the man? But those days were past.   Reddi was now proclaiming that the organisation had been "brought down with the tipping of a 27-year-old lad as the future Prime Minister. *Vinashkale vipareet buddhi* (When the time for destruction comes the brain goes topsy-turvy)."[5]   Even her court jester, D.K. Barooah, now winced at his famous "Indira is India" epigram.

But luckily for Mrs Gandhi there were still some Congress leaders around to proclaim, "Indira is here, the Congress is here, the country is here." Those were the words of Dr Chenna Reddy to greet the President of the "real" Congress. There was Tarkeshwari Sinha, still with her, to recite her Urdu verses to damn Reddi; there was the youth leader, Lalit Makan, still with Sanjay, to ask why human beings should not be worshipped in a country where images of stone and clay were worshipped. He was still on their side to declare that "we will worship Indira Gandhi."

One of Mrs Gandhi's supporters, Bhagwat Jha Azad, had claimed that 103 MPs, 210 former MPs, 197 members of State Assemblies and in all 347 of the 664 AICC members attended the convention which opened on New Year's day.

But B.P. Maurya, who along with Devaraj Urs was one of the main organisers of the convention, was now free to put the record straight. "All the figures announced at that time were bogus. The number of AICC members was not more than 112 and the number of sitting members from both houses of Parliament was about 16 or 17. It was we who made all the other bogus delegates. I had got all my followers of the RPI days and Devaraj Urs had brought a big group from Karnataka. . . ."

Blunt that he was, Maurya told Mrs Gandhi soon after the split, "Madam, I made you the President unconstitutionally and now you make me the general secretary of the party constitutionally."

"Yes, yes, I'll do it," Mrs Gandhi had told him, but he could see that she had already started acting high and mighty. It was, however, the Congress (I) victory in the "two-and-a-half States" that put her back on a high horse. "I am the only Opposition," Mrs Gandhi declared[6] in what looked like a return to her Emergency temper. Her literary agents were already writing on her "reincarnation."

Maurya had done hard campaigning for the party in Andhra Pradesh and had succeeded in getting many of his old supporters into the Assembly. He himself was hoping to get elected to the Rajya Sabha from Andhra Pradesh and had even bought 10 acres of land there in order to become eligible to contest from the State. Elections to the Rajya Sabha were to be held soon after the results of the Assembly elections. When Mrs Gandhi started allocating her party tickets for the Upper House, Maurya went and told her that he would like to get elected to the Rajya Sabha.

"She thought I wanted to get elected from Uttar Pradesh and immediately told me, 'No no, you don't come to the Rajya Sabha. I want to come to the Rajya Sabha'. By all means, I told her. She at once called Kamlapati Tripathi and also told him not to file his nomination for the Rajya Sabha as she herself wanted to be elected from Uttar Pradesh. But it so happened that her name was missing from the electoral list. It was just not there. I think Yashpal Kapoor must have played some mischief, and got her name removed from both Allahabad and Rae Bareli." Mrs Gandhi was furious but there was nothing she could do about it.

A few days later Maurya went to Mrs Gandhi again and asked, "Madam, what have you thought about me?"

"What about you?" she asked with a frown.

"About my coming to the Rajya Sabha, Madam," said Maurya.

"Mauryaji, not now!" she told him impatiently.

Maurya's patience, too, was over. He told her firmly, "Madam, I have only come to tell you that I am coming to the Rajya Sabha

[6]In a radio interview broadcast by the Australian Broadcasting Commission on 27 February 1978.

and I don't need your help. I am going to be elected from Andhra Pradesh."

Maurya left for Hyderabad, but before he reached there Mrs Gandhi had already talked to Dr Chenna Reddy on the phone. Not the person to brook any defiance, she wanted Reddy to stop Maurya from getting elected to the Rajya Sabha. But Chenna Reddy himself was on Maurya's side; he was grateful for the role Maurya had played in his becoming the Chief Minister.

After the party's victory in the Assembly elections, Maurya had suggested to Mrs Gandhi that at least one of the three States must have a Chief Minister belonging to the Scheduled Caste, for it was the all-out support of the Harijans which had been largely responsible for the party's victory.

"This is not possible," Mrs Gandhi told him. Then Maurya, too, started playing his cards. Here is the story in his own words:

"Devaraj Urs also did not trust Mrs Gandhi. Without waiting for a decision of the Parliamentary Board he collected his MLAs and got himself declared elected as the leader. But Dr Chenna Reddy did not have a majority with him. I knew he was opposed to Mrs Gandhi, and so when she did not agree to have a Scheduled Caste Chief Minister, I proposed the name of Chenna Reddy. She flared up and said, 'No, no, he is a very dangerous man. He is not at all dependable.' She even used certain bad words about his character and integrity. But I was equally adamant, and said, 'No, no, we have to fight Brahmanand Reddi and even Neelam Sanjeeva Reddy is not with you. There must be some Reddy and it is only Dr Chenna Reddy.' She kept saying no, no, no.

"Chenna Reddy telephoned me at midnight and said 'Mauryaji, I want to know what this woman is going to do for me.' I said you leave it to me, you will be the Chief Minister. But Reddy said. 'No, no, no, it is your view. I want to know the view of Indira Gandhi.' She is not for you, I told him, to which he said, 'Go and tell her that I am Dr Chenna Reddy, I know how to fight my enemy.' I went to her house right then, although it was past midnight. Her security men said she was already asleep but I told them to go and tell her I had come for an urgent work. She came out, saying what is it? what is it? I told her the exact words Chenna Reddy had used, and said if she did not agree to make him the Chief Minister it would be very difficult to control him. She looked worried and said, 'Why don't you go and call Narasimha Rao?' So I drove to

the house of Narasimha Rao,[7] woke him up and took him with me
to her house. We started discussing the matter, but Rao kept hedg-
ing for he was himself an aspirant for the chief ministership. Then
she telephoned another Andhra leader, Raja Ram, but he too
seemed to be a candidate himself. It was already around 1.30 or 2
a.m. and we were in an *impasse*. Then she started saying, 'Nothing
doing, nothing doing, Mauryaji wants Chenna Reddy, he is
pressurizing me. All right, let it be that way...' And so it was that
Chenna Reddy became the Chief Minister. He was very nice to me
when I told him I wanted to be elected to the Rajya Sabha. He
allotted the entire Cabinet to me and so I came to the Rajya
Sabha.''

Maurya's name had gone into her black list. But a sharper
confrontation came some time later. With Mrs Gandhi's "reincarnation" the son too was trying hard to rise. Obviously pressed by
Sanjay Gandhi and his supporters who were regathering, Mrs
Gandhi came up with the idea at one of the Working Committee
meetings to give the Youth Congress equal status to the Congress
(I). She said she was keen to make it an autonomous organisation
with separate funds and working independently of the Congress (I).

Maurya shot up to say that this would be a "suicidal step." He
said he believed that at least 50 per cent of the Congress debacle
in 1977 had been because of the Youth Congress.

"I don't agree," Mrs Gandhi said angrily.

"You may or may not agree, Madam," said Maurya, "but it is
a fact. I repeat that 50 per cent of our defeat was because of the
Youth Congress and if you give autonomous status to the Youth
Congress it would be suicidal for the party."

"Then I would prefer to ask the youths not to organise themselves," Mrs Gandhi shot back.

"You may do that, Madam," said Maurya. Nobody in the
Working Committee was saying a word. It was all a dialogue between the two.

"I would prefer to work with the youth," said Mrs Gandhi.

"Yes, you can work with the youth and we will work in the
Congress."

Mrs Gandhi burst forth: "Today I am popular not because of

[7]A former Chief Minister of Andhra Pradesh (1971-73) and a prominent
supporter of Mrs Gandhi.

anyone of you sitting in this room. I am popular on my own...."

But Maurya too was not to be cowed so easily. He said: "Madam, you may be popular on your own, but this notion is very wrong, I can illustrate to you how best we have contributed to your popularity in our own styles...."

Nobody except Sanat Mehta from Gujarat even protested against Mrs Gandhi's remarks. "Don't humiliate us all," Mehta had said. He must have been shocked that she had forgotten all that he and his friends had done for her during her Gujarat visit only some months earlier.

That very afternoon several MLAs from Andhra Pradesh had gone and told Maurya that they had sought an appointment with Mrs Gandhi but she had refused to see them. Some of them had been Ministers in the Vengal Rao Government and had resigned at Mrs Gandhi's behest. Maurya met Mrs Gandhi in the evening and asked her if the Andhra MLAs had sought an interview with her.

"Yes, they did," she said.

"And they say you refused to meet them."

"That's right," she said.

"But why, Madam? Didn't they help you when you were in need?"

Maurya had got used to talking frankly with her, for that was the kind of free relationship that had developed between them since her defeat. But her new attitude surprised him. "If you pressurize me I shall resign from the party," she said in anger.

"I am not pressurizing you Madam, I am only requesting you."

"No, no, in the Working Committee also you were trying to do the same. I'll not be dictated by anybody."

"I am only submitting, Madam...."

She cut him short with a curt "no, no" and walked out.

It indeed was a sort of "reincarnation." Her great empire had shrunk to two-and-a-half States and half a party, but she was an Empress again!

V

SON'S POLITICAL REBIRTH

The apartment was too well known to Sanjay Gandhi. It had been one of his favourite pleasure haunts in those golden days when he had only to nod to get things done. Though the place belonged to a business friend, it was for all practical purposes his own. He knew every nook and corner of it. But that day the setting of the hall was very different. Instead of the sofas and the divans and the arty bric-a-brac there lay all the paraphernalia of a religious ceremony: incense, camphor, sandalwood, and bang in the middle where the centre table used to lie there was a blazing *havan kund*, with pundits chanting *mantras* around it. A *yajna* was on.

It was all a cover for an important meeting that the businessman had planned for Sanjay Gandhi, within a week of his mother's fall. The sudden change in the country had left them stunned. Sanjay had never felt so low before. Some of his best friends had deserted him. Kuldip Narang, his old partner in many of his escapades and widely known as one of his links with the CIA during the Emergency, had fled to America. Even his Doon School chum, Kamal Nath, who had led the toughs to Amethi, had flown out of the country. He was assailed by fears of what the Janata might do to him. The very idea of languishing in a dark cell was horrifying, but a possibility all the same. It was a time when he would clutch at any straw.

The idea had come from his business chum: Why not meet Kanti

Desai? He was the new "Sanjay" on the Indian scene. There couldn't be a more useful friend on the Janata side than him. They felt they could count on Kanti's greed, perhaps he could understand Sanjay's predicament better than any other man. It was important not only for Sanjay, but for his business friend too; everybody knew how well the man had feathered his nest during the Emergency. And so Kanti was going to be the "chief guest" at the *yajna*. It was not a particularly clever plan; the camouflage was all too clear. But then you needed to create a situation in which the meeting did not appear contrived.

Sanjay had been shy and nervous, but there was his business friend to do the talking on his behalf. Very much a man of the trade himself, Kanti was easy to get along with, especially for a businessman. There was not much need for dissembling between them, for they were basically of the same stuff, driven by the same urges and motivations. And they were not asking Kanti for much, were they? Only to smoothen the attitude of his father towards Sanjay who had suddenly fallen among enemies. Everyone was aware of the tremendous influence Kanti had on his father, an influence which could perhaps only be matched with that of Sanjay on his mother. That hard and inflexible mind could only bend by the sweet reasoning of his son, for Morarji was like a hard glacier and Kanti the gentle sunbeam under whose mild pressure his puritanism would melt. Kanti was not averse to it, but...Of course, that was understood. Everything has a price. According to one version, a good part of the eighty lakhs which Kanti Desai contributed to the Janata fund for the Assembly elections in June 1977 came from the "Save Sanjay Deal."

But to soften his father was one thing, to save Sanjay Gandhi from his troubles quite another. Cases soon cropped up here, there, everywhere. The most troublesome, and the one that Sanjay Gandhi feared most was *Kissa Kursi Ka* case. He knew that would take a real legal battle to get over. In June 1977, he flew off to Bombay along with his wife, Maneka, giving rise to widespread suspicion that they were trying to flee the country. But those were "just plain rumours," according to Khushwant Singh,[1] the then Editor of *The Illustrated Weekly*, who played their friend, philosopher and guide during their stay in Bombay. Sanjay's primary mission, said Singh,

---

[1] In an interview with the author.

was to meet the eminent lawyer, Nani Palkhiwala, and see if he would accept his brief. Nani, they knew, would be a hard nut to crack, for he had shown no hesitation at all in dropping Mrs Gandhi's case when she was at the height of her power. But possibly Khushwant, an old friend of the celebrated lawyer, could influence him to take up Sanjay's case. Khushwant took them to Nani, who had met them with the most disarming courtesy. And then Khushwant had broached the subject. Himself trained as a barrister, Khushwant had put forth his defence of Sanjay, hoping that this might persuade Nani to accept the brief. But the lawyer had gone cold. "Please don't ask me to do this," he had told Khushwant with polite firmness. The rejection must have been maddening for the egotistical young man, but there was little that could be done. Not everybody was Khushwant.

Maneka Gandhi had gone to J.P. under the cover of a journalist. Though the ostensible purpose was to interview the old man for her magazine, *Surya*, her real objective was clear to all, from the very questions she had to ask, and the way she asked them. Not that it was improper in any way to want to know where Mrs Gandhi had gone wrong, what she ought to do and so on. If Mrs Gandhi was her mother-in-law and she herself a journalist who could be blamed for that but providence? But there was no mistaking the fact that the "journalist" was trying to win the sympathy of J.P. for the Gandhi family. The sick old man had shifted and groaned at the prospect of having to supply reasonable answers that neither sounded biased, nor seemed opposed to his defunct "total revolution." She asked him what he had to say about the constant harassment which the Gandhi family was being subjected to, the censoring of letters, bugging of phones, always being followed.... The allusion was clear— who were these people he had brought to power, and did he now condone them for the very things which had made the Emergency the ugly thing it was? "It was a hangover of the Emergency," he had replied.[2] Objectionable as it was, the Janata Government, he said, were at best victims of a trend that had been set before. When Maneka had wanted to know about Mrs Gandhi's future, he had replied that she could at least have expressed her regret for what had happened. No, to take the responsibility was a brave thing to do no doubt, but to be sorry and admit publicly that a disaster had

[2] In *Surya*, August 1977.

taken place causing much harm to the country was another matter again. That sort of selfless and self-effacing attitude was what was needed. Instead, the brave posture she had affected had only shaken his faith in her belief in democracy. To Maneka's significant question, put deliberately in her girlish way, as to what Mrs Gandhi should do to come back, J.P. had offered the familiar platitudes such as "she must serve the people, however possible...function as a political leader, however possible"... And what had she been doing all along if not serving the people 'however possible'?

J.P. was still powerful. Surely, the man who could rouse the whole country against her so dramatically could just as easily keep the wheel from turning full circle. The wheel of fire, on which all highfalutin' ideas would be tested and then burnt. The whole thing was absurd like a Restoration Comedy. Everyone was saying the same thing over and over, for there was precious little anyone could do. The same interests and passions in men had made them run after one another like sworn enemies.

Her insecurity drove her to yet another refuge—this time a Tantrik. Human reason had failed. No one could change your stars if the ones you were born under insisted on being bad. But the Tantrik thought otherwise. The stars may not be susceptible to change, but the evil could be washed away. The price for this was exorbitant, but so was the enormity of the evil that had accumulated. Of course, it wasn't going to be easy at all. The *yajna* would cost, but it could be relied upon. Apart from washing all the evil away, it would bring Sanjay to the top again. He would become the Deputy Prime Minister by 1984—shades of Orwell's *1984*. The gods would see to that, as long as she managed the terrestrial part of the affair. He would buy the gods on her behalf. Having done her part, Maneka waited with her fingers crossed.

And the mother all the while kept on with her opposing statements about the son who had inherited all her fears and arrogance and none of her charisma. Mrs Gandhi may have been conscious of it when she had insisted that her son had leadership qualities and had denied, in the same breath, that politics was his forte. In her conversations with an American writer, Mary C. Carras,[3] the doting mother's mind came through:

Mrs G : Anti-Sanjay has nothing to do with the car project. It was

[3]In *Indira Gandhi : In the Crucible of Leadership.*

because, I think, he showed leadership qualities.

Carras: You feel he did show leadership qualities?

Mrs G: Definitely he did—in organising the Youth Congress. There is no doubt about it. He has character and discipline. And a mind with regard to problems. He's not literary. He enthused our young people, got them thinking on constructive lines, working with dedication. He built up the Youth Congress in a short time and it was very well organized.

Carras: But he has alienated a lot of people in the process.

Mrs G: No. It was only the propaganda. This was a clean business. He could have made money—say, like Kanti Desai—doing nothing. But people who have met him—take the lawyers on his case—have the highest opinion of him. And certainly nobody who didn't have character would have faced this situation with the dignity he has shown. . . .What was very wrong was the publicity he got. And it was wrong to lionize him. He and I were actually embarrassed. I didn't know for some time. I never listen to radio or see TV. He drew my attention to it and asked if it was necessary. And then I spoke to the I and B people. They said they couldn't stop it immediately because people would say the Opposition had done it.

Carras: Do you see a political role for him in the future?

Mrs G: He is not basically interested in politics. . .in fact, he wouldn't have been in politics at all but for the criticism and tremendous attack on him. He wanted to stand for Parliament because he felt that only he could reply to the false allegations.

Carras: But you do think he has leadership qualities? Therefore, you must see some sort of role for him.

Mrs G: Not necessarily in politics. What I mean by leadership is he is a good organiser.

But it was just like Mrs Gandhi to remark elsewhere, "My son, Sanjay, has not and will not leave politics." Sanjay was a good organiser, true, but just like those brats who carried off those underhand deals behind thick veils of money and influence. It was Jawaharlal Nehru who had first described them as "brats"—upper class boys whose pastime it was to steal cars and scooters—recognisable sores of high society who danced away their nights in discos, and never in their lives had to fret for lack of diversions. In such an atmosphere of nonchalant affluence did the son grow—the dummies around him, all in his own image, knowing perfectly each whim and fancy of their master. Hopes of profit made them unite into little groups all over the country. It was like a hierarchy, Sanjay looking down from the top of the ladder. Word travelled downwards to the lowest members, who seemed ever more anxious to please, for the less you had the more you craved for. As Russell once put it, man is gregarious because he is selfish. Just take all those advantages from Sanjay Gandhi, take away his upper class background, for instance, and then watch the whole pyramid come crumbling down. If such a day came to pass and Mrs Gandhi were to she it, she would realize how all the youth rallies got organised as though they had a life of their own.

Sanjay and his mother were like two sides of a record—the songs were different, but the themes and the voices were the same. Her morbid attachment to Sanjay was based on fear and a long-drawn sense of guilt. Her own father couldn't spare time for her mother and her relationship with Feroze was anything but normal. If her father had groomed her to be the Prime Minister one day, it seemed only natural to her to keep the dynastic principle going. Their sense of insecurity was the strongest bond between mother and son, the only one which made her defence of him relentless to the point of raving. Neither could see beyond the charmed circle of sycophants. They both needed them equally strongly for about the same reasons. The very possibility that Sanjay should prove disloyal to her was enough to give her a shudder. "I think even Sanjay is not loyal to her," B.P. Maurya told me. "She does not trust anyone." Those who flocked around her were aware how essential their praise of her son was for her psychic survival. Whether it was Siddhartha Shankar Ray or Brahmanand Reddi or indeed Dev Kant Barooah, they had all kept her illusions alive with their fawning. This had finally reassured Mrs Gandhi that Sanjay was more sinned against than sinning. So the men kept humouring her, some because they had been partners in her crime and had simply no choice, like Bansi Lal and V.C.Shukla, others like Vasant Sathe who were themselves so overwhelmed by her charisma that they were certain it would have to be the touchstone of their success. "Sathe is a very cunning fellow," remarked Maurya. "He is cunning like me. He thinks she has great mass appeal and he can utilize her. But he is mistaken. It is she who will utilize him, not he her. He is in as much illusion as I was."

Let her lead them, thought her supporters, and let them supply her with the fuel to feed her illusions—her strength lay in them and in her continued strength lay their hopes. A veritable web of deceptions, a burlesque tragedy in which all the characters were alike, milder versions of the protagonist. In their eyes she could see the hope that she believed the country saw in hers. And yet she had trusted no one. Her egotism made this impossible. And now she could not even be condemned, only pitied when you saw what had brought out this distrust in her of everyone who had helped her lurch forward—for those who fed her illusions by the same token destroyed whatever faith she had in them. Here was the contradiction that explained the tall ladder pointing upward to glory. Not all the rungs were there. She had gone dropping them as she climbed.

Just as Mrs Gandhi landed at the airport in Delhi on 5 May 1978, after an intense campaign in Azamgarh—her first successful attempt to salvage a constituency in her home State—she got the news of Sanjay's arrest. He was in jail. The Supreme Court was satisfied that he had abused his liberty by attempting to suborn prosecution witnesses and had forfeited his right to be free. He had then surrendered before the Additional Sessions Judge and had been remanded to jail custody for a month. During the 50 minutes she was with Sanjay, Mrs Gandhi told him: "Never mind, my son, this is your political rebirth." To boost his morale, she had taken her political supporters and an American lawyer from California—"perhaps he was Nixon's defence lawyer," a local wit had remarked.

In spite of the brave front Mrs Gandhi put up, she was obviously rattled by her son's arrest. The victory in Azamgarh gave her a new confidence, but with this came rumours that she herself might be arrested again. With renewed vigour she set out to make her party a more fitting instrument for the "national purpose" she envisaged for it : to wage a countrywide battle for mother and son whose throne had been usurped. As she had told Barbara Bourne, a journalist from Oslo, she was "chosen to rule India" and her election defeat was only a "nightmare" that would soon be over.[4]

As a preliminary to the real battle that lay ahead, Mrs Gandhi had directed her party to organize a massive resistance in the event of her arrest. What came as a new ray of hope, however, was the fresh trouble brewing in the Janata Party. Charan Singh, the Home Minister, had moved to a hospital, there to ruminate over his growing differences with Morarji Desai. A nice way to convalesce. He had done it many times before; whenever a strong political crisis had thrown him out of gear he had retired sulkily to his sick bed to dream of action ahead. And now from the hospital he had fired his salvo at the Janata colleagues. They were breaking up the party and encouraging dissidence in the States where his men ruled.

The old man's anger had stirred Mrs Gandhi into hopeful speculation and she had dispatched an emissary to the hospital forthwith. The *National Herald,* her very own mouthpiece, surprisingly came out with the details of the tete-a-tete between the emissary, Bhisma Narain Singh and Charan Singh. The Home Minister had been in a surly, rejecting mood until Bhisma Narain had turned up with a lovely looking bouquet from the lady who wished him speedy recovery. The political speculation that it might have caused was the only hitch that had discouraged Mrs Gandhi from coming to the hospital herself, the emissary informed Charan Singh. "She is my daughter, she is always welcome," the overwhelmed old man had said, but as though to warn her not to take his words too literally, he had hastily added, "These political things don't matter."

It was quite a change, though for those who remembered Charan Singh's snub to Mrs Gandhi in similar circumstances when the Janata Government was still young. That time Mrs Gandhi had come back fuming from her meeting with the Home Minister. "Mauryaji, what sort of man is he—this Chaudhary Saheb?" she had asked. What had happened? Maurya wanted to know. Well, said Mrs Gandhi, her only crime had been to request Charan Singh not to persecute her and Sanjay. "I requested him not to have commissions of inquiry against me and Sanjay. After all, we had already received enough punishment from the electorate, I told him, but he never even acknowledged my request. He was all the time so proud!"

Emboldened by the growing internal squabbles in the Janata Government and its swiftly declining credibility, Mrs Gandhi chose 9 August to observe "Save India Day" on a massive scale. But it turned out to be a poor show, partly due to the obvious lack of enthusiasm on the part of the people and partly due to rain, which made a Delhi Editor to observe, "Judging from the limited turn-out in the capital and elsewhere, not many people shared Mrs Gandhi's view on the urgent need to save India, especially if it is raining." What had meant to be a mass protest fizzled out into a mere damp squib. "So deep was the determination to 'Save India'," commented Arun Shourie, "that a few hours of rain made them postpone the 'saving' of their dear and beloved motherland to another day."

The whole exercise had obviously been more of a "Save Indira Day." Its only achievement was the piles of forms filled up by members of the Sanjay brigade saying: "I... resident of... believe that the Shah Commission is politically motivated and that any action which the Janata Government will take against our leader and President, Smt. Indira Gandhi, will be strongly condemned in a non-violent manner by the path shown by Mahatma Gandhi. I solemnly pledge to court arrest as a sign of solidarity and support to our beloved leader, Smt. Indira Gandhi." Many chose, however, to spend the day differently. Dozens of people turned up in heavy rain at 12 Willingdon Crescent shouting "Save India from Indira." They distributed pamphlets describing her as a "political criminal" and a "fake socialist," but they got beaten up by the Sanjay goons.

Sanjay, after all, was only doing what he had told the Tantrik he planned to do. Neither Dhirendra Brahmachari nor R. K. Dhawan would let the Tantrik in, but he had been called by Maneka, and Sanjay insisted on being apprised of the latest from the gods. Sanjay was curious to know if his plans would succeed. But the clever Tantrik turned the question on him: what were his plans for the future? Came the precocious reply in no uncertain terms. Why, he would create a law and order problem in the country. He needed no convincing that it was the shortest path to glory, and he must get it, for he considered it his birthright.

A rather flattering report by Dadayut Abdel Nabi, an Egyptian diplomatic correspondent, described Rajiv Gandhi as a "gentleman." She was on an Indian Airlines plane captained by Rajiv. Being of the pushing sort, she managed a word with him, and arranged an interview with his mother. Full of praise for Rajiv, she seemed to echo the countless others who had painfully emphasised the contrast between the two brothers—Sanjay, taciturn, distrustful and unpopular, and Rajiv, shy, sensitive and 'correct'. "They are all agreed on one thing in India," she wrote, "mainly that if she abandoned her son she could sweep everything before her without rival or competitor." But then all those who understood Mrs Gandhi knew how naive it was to attribute the mother's failure to the intransigence of her son. The moment you made a distinction which marked them off as two separate individuals, you established the fallacy of the argument.

All the former satraps of Mrs Gandhi, like Zail Singh, Jagannath Mishra and N. D. Tewari, turned up at the Tees Hazari courts to give moral support to Sanjay and V. C. Shukla on the day of judgment in the *Kissa Kursi Ka* case. In his 362-page verdict, the Sessions Judge had said: "All the facts would lead to the inference of the existence of a conspiracy between Mr V. C. Shukla and Mr Sanjay Gandhi and also to the inference of abetment by one in regard to the commissions of offences mentioned in the charges." The charges framed against them stood established "beyond reasonable doubts." Sanjay's hoodlums shouted "hai, hai," some even tried to mob N. K. Singh of the CBI who had investigated the case and Ram Jethamalani, the Special Prosecutor for the CBI. Minor scuffles followed.

Next morning, Sanjay and Shukla were sentenced to two years' rigorous imprisonment and a fine of Rs 10,000 and Rs 25,000 respectively. But the Judge suspended both the fine and the sentences until 26 March 1979, releasing them on bail till then. When Sanjay's hoodlums started shouting yet again, the Judge observed, "I do believe that one should not become sentimental. I love one (of the convicts) as my son and the other as my brother. I have acted as a judge." At this Sanjay retorted from the dock: "I hope what you say you really believe." As though this were a sign for them to display their heroism, the supporters plunged into action, abusing the police officers and the prosecutors. Someone hurled a CBI register and a copy of the Criminal Procedure Code towards the dais amid a chorus of "*Jab tak suraj chand rahega, Sanjay tera naam rahega.*"

The funniest things were happening. A windfall from Sydney came just the next day with the death of one Mrs Ruth Cowell, a long-time admirer of Jawaharlal Nehru. A pious lady, she obviously did not think that a saint and a sinner could carry the same blood in their veins. She had left Nehru's grandson her beach-side property in suburban Sydney worth $100,000.

By this time a strong demand had come up in the Congress (I) for the return of the young master so that he could give new life to the party. The party office sent out a press release which carried a member's plea: "It is only possible under his (Sanjay Gandhi's) leadership that a strong Congress can emerge to combat the growing militant force of RSS which poses a serious threat to all norms of democracy."

Soon after came reports of Sanjay's meetings with Raj Narain. While Raj Narain said he didn't think the meetings were at all politically significant, Sanjay told his wife's magazine in an interview[5] that he did not want to embarrass his new friend by revealing all they had discussed.

While the "single-point programme" of this odd friendship was just beginning to take shape, Sanjay Gandhi was displaying his 'character and dignity' on the streets of Delhi. On 1 May, he led an assorted band of hoodlums to the Janpath which became for a while the scene of a pitched battle between his unruly mob and the police. P. R. S. Brar, the deputy commissioner of police, described how a brick had landed on his ear-lobe. Sanjay had rushed forward, ordering his men to beat Brar up. "*Maro isko,*" he had shouted. This was all that was needed for the mob to rough him up. When police tried to arrest him, Sanjay majestically squatted on the ground and refused to move (Raj Narain style!) into the van. People were horrified to see a tempo filled with bricks and soda-water bottles in the Sanjay procession. In Lok Sabha, several members conferred the title of the "leader of goondas and vagabonds" on Sanjay Gandhi, but C.M Stephen was there to correct them. The procession was peaceful and non-violent, he declared in true Gandhian style. Within days huge posters appeared all about the city showing the great hero crouching before police lathis. His "political rebirth" was complete!

[5]*Surya,* July 1979.

VI

MP FROM CHIKMAGALUR

With her son still in jail, and her first Lok Sabha seat from Uttar Pradesh in her bag, Mrs Gandhi had gone for a holiday to Karnataka, the State she still ruled. She had chosen Nandi Hills, a holiday resort about 55 miles north of Bangalore. There on 27 May 1978 she had called Devaraj Urs, Dr Chenna Reddy and Nasikrao Tirpude, a Congress (I) Minister in Maharashtra, for a 'summit' meeting, ostensibly to discuss the party programme in the three States. It was during this meeting that it was decided that Mrs Gandhi would get into one of the two houses of Parliament.

Only a few days earlier, on 24 May, she had allegedly filed a declaration in the Electoral Registration Office seeking enrolment as a voter in the Doddaballapur taluk of Bangalore district. She had claimed in an affidavit that she was an "ordinary resident" at Vishnu Ashram, situated at the foothills of Nandi Hills. The Ashram belonged to Swami Satchidananda, who had been a secretary to Chief Minister Urs. There was very little of a 'swami' in this thin, sprightly man, who had once worked for a Bangalore newspaper before attaching himself to K. Hanumanthaiya, then a Minister at the Centre, after which he got tagged to Devaraj Urs. Even so, Satchidananda had set up an Ashram which gave him the right to be called a 'Swami.' Urs had sent him to the Rajya Sabha, and he was only too willing to step down to make way for Mrs Gandhi, who was anxious to somehow enter Parliament. She had first planned to get into the Rajya Sabha from Uttar Pradesh, but that had been thwarted by her own cronies who had managed to get her name removed from the electoral rolls in the State.

To get elected to the Lok Sabha, she didn't have to be a resident of Karnataka, but to get into the Upper House she would have needed some kind of local credentials, which she had sought by claiming to be a resident of the Vishnu Ashram. But as was alleged later, a Revenue Inspector who had been sent to make an on-the-spot check of the claim had gone back and reported that the Ashram was not the permanent residence of Mrs Gandhi, and that was the end to yet another effort to get into Parliament. Of course, Mrs Gandhi's supporters gave an entirely different explanation. They said it was they who had convinced Mrs Gandhi that there was no need for her to go to the Rajya Sabha, that it would be *infra dig* for a leader of her stature. She could as easily get elected to the Lok Sabha, and they had even hunted out a safe seat for her—Chikmagalur (literally, 'town of little daughter'), a sleepy, coffee-rich constituency, nearly 1500 miles away from Delhi. The name had rung a bell in Mrs Gandhi's mind. Wasn't it the same place where she had been forced to take shelter behind riot shields in November 1977? It was indeed the same constituency, but her supporters, Gundu Rao, F.M. Khan, Jaffer Sharief and others had done their best to convince her that it was the safest seat possible and if the sitting MP, Chandra Gowda had won by over 50,000 votes in 1977, she would win by at least two lakh votes. Apart from being comfortably tucked away in the backwaters, Chikmagalur had nearly 42 per cent of its population living below the poverty line, just the sort of people who would lap her up as their Messiah, their "Indramma." She had agreed.

Devaraj Urs knew Mrs Gandhi was considering Chikmagalur as a possible constituency to contest from, but surprisingly he himself was somewhat taken aback when the first announcement came. It was his Minister, Gundu Rao, who broke the news in Bangalore, something that was bound to hurt the pride of Urs. If anybody was to have the credit for getting Mrs Gandhi returned to Parliament it had to be him. But Gundu Rao, the ambitious, tough-talking leader of the Sanjay caucus in Karnataka had his own dreams. He was trying to become not just a parallel centre of authority in the State but even aspired to dislodge Urs from the chief ministership. He had done more than anybody else to create bad blood between Mrs Gandhi and Urs, by carrying all manner of tales against him.

Even during the Emergency, Gundu Rao had tried to steel a march over his Chief Minister by extending an invitation to the 'rising son of India' to grace Bangalore with his visit. Urs was initially scornful but he was too practical to go against the tide. On second thoughts, he had not only considered it wise to receive Sanjay Gandhi himself but had gone out of his way to make the reception as lavish and grand as possible. Only after a few meetings with Sanjay Gandhi, Urs even told a press conference how very impressed he was by the young man. He laid it on thick by saying that Sanjay Gandhi was even cleverer than his mother, that he had a deeper insight into men and matters and could make a "mature political leader." A clever politician if ever there was one, Urs thought nothing of doing a little buttering on the side if it helped his political ambitions. In the early days of his climb, he was even known to have sent fresh vegetables by air for Uma Shankar Dixit and Yashpal Kapoor—he was still courting the courtiers.

But when it came to fawning around the young master, he could not beat his younger colleague, for while Urs had become conscious of his position, Gundu Rao did not hesitate to cringe and flatter openly. So impressed was Sanjay Gandhi by the devotion of Gundu Rao that he pressed Urs to promote him from Minister of State to the rank of a full Minister. Though Urs was later to disclaim that he had any idea that Sanjay Gandhi used to throw his weight around, he had himself had the experience of it too well. After Gundu Rao had wormed his way into the confidence of Sanjay Gandhi, he not only started ignoring Urs but even began making public display of how little he bothered about the Chief Minister.

Urs himself once told a confidant how Gundu Rao used to go out of his way to insult him. On one occasion both of them were staying at the Karnataka Bhawan in New Delhi. Urs had wanted to discuss something with him and had sent for him. When Gundu Rao did not come, he once again sent a messenger to his room, but still he didn't come. Finally Urs himself went to Gundu Rao's room. You just ignored my messages, he told him lightly, but Gundu Rao retorted: "Don't forget I am not your Minister, I am Sanjay Gandhi's Minister." Urs had swallowed it.

It must have been his pent-up anger against the pressures of the Sanjay men which made him refer repeatedly to Sanjay Gandhi during the CWC (I) meeting in March 1978. As though rebutting the fears expressed by some of the members about the reemergence of Sanjay Gandhi, he said there was a clear understanding with Mrs Gandhi that Sanjay was no longer in politics and that he would have nothing to do with the affairs of the party. Surely Mrs Gandhi could not have liked the point being rubbed in. At a press conference soon after the meeting, Urs had made no secret of his resentment against the efforts of some members of the Sanjay caucus to influence the choice of Ministers in his State. His Council of Ministers, he had remarked laconically, would be "finalized in Bangalore, not in Delhi" and reporters had not missed the touch of sarcasm in his remark that "I am Devaraj Urs, she is Mrs Gandhi." He had tried to give the whole thing a different twist by explaining that their experiences on Centre-State relations differed vastly—"we have certain experiences which she may not have." But he had gone on to say that the spectacular triumph of the Congress (I) in the Karnataka Assembly elections should not be attributed to "one single person." Nobody could miss the import of that remark. When asked if it was unethical on the part of Mrs Gandhi to have used the Emergency to build up Sanjay, he said: "Yes, that was why we suffered defeat in March last year in the elections to Lok Sabha." Though Urs tried to make amends within days by declaring that Mrs Gandhi was his leader, the seeds of discord had been laid.

Both Mrs Gandhi and Urs were at Kadur, a Janata Party stronghold in the Chikmagalur constituency, on 28 October. The allegedly fraudulent affidavit had already been exposed by a Janata MP, Era Sezhiyan, in Delhi a few days earlier. But that day the charge had become graver by the revelation made in Delhi that Mrs Gandhi had not applied for the deletion of her name as voter from the electoral roll in New Delhi Parliamentary constituency while seeking enorlment in Karnataka. J. B. Kripalani, who said he had seen the certified copy of the affidavit, wondered how a person belonging to the distinguished family of patriots with a saintly mother like Kamala should "stoop to such mean devices" to secure a seat in the Rajya Sabha."[1] The news from Delhi had fouled the air for her. She had planned to go on for hectic campaigning along with Devaraj Urs, but instead they had a rather brief and acrimonious meeting and the Chief Minister had walked out of the room red in the face.

[1]*The Times of India*, 29 October 1978.

He had driven back to Bangalore, but before starting he had sent a message to his headquarters to arrange for a press conference at the West-End Hotel next afternoon. It was conjectured that the Chief Minister had been blamed by Mrs Gandhi for the whole blotch-up of the declaration, and that he might come out with some home truths at the press conference. He did nothing of the sort, however, and talked the whole time about inconsequential things, so that the reporters wondered if there was any need to call a press conference at all. But some of the confidants of the Chief Minister knew better. Clearly there was no love lost between the two. Even the idea of sabotaging her elections had crossed his mind, but only briefly. His well-wishers had cautioned him that her defeat would really mean his defeat. He had plunged himself vigorously into the campaign. Until the elections, at least, Mrs Gandhi's interest also lay in having him on her right side. No matter how safe the constituency, his help might come in handy, as indeed it did in the end. But as the campaign progressed, it became clear to all that her trust in him was begin- ning to wane. There was Pranab Mukherjee, her trusted Minister for Banking during the Emergency, managing the lady's war chest, and Yashpal Kapoor was still very much around.

After filing her nomination at the time given by her astrologers, Mrs Gandhi had driven straight to the Dharmasthala to propitiate the gods. Her campaign style was flamboyant as usual. Two youths would first come zooming on their motorbikes with the news that Mrs Gandhi was coming to address the meeting. After a while the motorcade would arrive, with young men on motorbikes and Mrs Gandhi herself in a soft green Impala. At night, she would hold a lamp upon her face so that people could have a glimpse of her famous profile. Manifestly, she had lost none of her campaign wiles. A grand affair, it brought out all the latent drama in her to full public view. Her men had spread the word that this was not an ordinary campaign, it was the one that would clinch the issue of her come-back. They had gone around telling the simple folks that this was an election which would make Mrs Gandhi the Prime Minister again. There were even people who believed that "Indr- amma" was very much on the throne still. Just the kind to swallow the clever propaganda, the poor were awed dumb by the spectacle which surely would not lie. The noise made by her campaign drew all the attention to her. In her 18 days of phrenetic campaigning, she addressed nearly 160 poll meetings, apart from her 'padyatras.' Not one temple or math or church or mosque or *dargah* which fell on her way did she miss out. People noticed such things. A reporter following her campaign trail recorded that when a muezzin at a distant mosque intoned his call to the faithful, she stopped her meeting until the prayers were over. Amid her hectic tours, she had found time to pray atop the Baba Budan Hills.

All hypocrisy, cried George Fernandes, the only one who really lent life and vigour to the Janata campaign. He was excellent—out on the streets with a bucket in hand he went about collecting funds for the campaign, and in his speeches he seemed to relive the whole sordid drama of the Emergency. He stirred the emotions of the people with his gruesome descriptions of how his brother and mother were tortured by the police of Indira Gandhi—the "devil incarnate."

There was plenty to stir the feelings of the people even during the campaign. A college girl, Gayatri, was killed when police opened fire at Ujjire. Mark Tully of the BBC and Lawrence Malkin of the *Time* who saw it happen said the police lathi-charge and firing were unwarranted. Devaraj Urs asked for an inquiry into the incident and slowly the anger and revulsion died down once again to the beating of drums on both sides.

Mrs Gandhi's candidature had thrown the Janata Party into a paroxysm of nervousness. General Secretary Ramkrishna Hegde sent off frantic calls to all good men to come to the aid of the party in its "hour of peril." For it had come to that. The way the party went into a flap over selecting a suitable candidate to fight Mrs Gandhi was almost comical. At one stage they even thought of roping in Raj Kumar, the matinee idol of the South, to fight the lady, but he refused to be taken in. Veerendra Patil, clean but devoid of any charisma, was the best they could find. The other parties, too, had gone into a turmoil, especially the weak-willed and demoralised Congress, which was clearly riven into three distinct groups, those who were for defeating her, those who wanted her back and those who did not want to take any position at all. Threatened with the prospect of the party breaking up, the Parliamentary Board hastily decided to support her candidature, which showed that the pro-Indira section dominated the party. The Karnataka unit, however, defied the directive and issued a call to work for Mrs Gandhi's defeat. The party's only Chief Minister, A. K. Anthony, resigned in protest and Karan Singh, Chandrajeet Yadav quit the Working Committee. Even the pro-CPI elements in the Congress were split. One section led by K. R. Ganesh was openly campaigning for her. "She is again the rallying point for all progressive and democratic forces," wrote a political commentator with cutting irony.[2]

The CPI itself was in no less a quandary. Chairman Dange defied the party which had officially opposed her candidature. By publicly welcoming Mrs Gandhi's decision, Dange showed he was not the kind to let down an old comrade. So angry were his partymen in Bombay that for the first time they did not even observe the old man's birthday. At the other end of the political spectrum, there was the RSS Chief Balasaheb Deoras saying that his men would not come into the picture at all. Perhaps to keep in line with his "mercy petitions" from the jail, Deoras had for long been advocating a policy of "forgive and forget" towards the lady. Who could tell if some day the RSS were again to be at her mercy? There was nothing wrong in enlightened self-interest, was there? He would leave it to his Jan Sangh men to fight it out with her—another battle between dictatorship and democracy, as L. K. Advani called it. The Jat chieftain, Charan Singh was for the moment more furious against the Janata Government than against Mrs Gandhi, for the wounds Morarji Desai had inflicted on him were fresher. He had been "hounded out from the Government like a dog" as he put it himself, and it took a good deal of persuasion from his friends to make him issue a statement against Mrs Gandhi's candidature in Chikmagalur. Maintaining that the differences in the Janata Party were a "measure of its faith in internal democracy," the former Home Minister said Mrs Gandhi taking "advantage of the Janata Party's liberal policy lives in a palatial government building, moves about the country spreading falsehood, shows scant respect to courts and commissions and even justifies her infamous act of Emergency."

As it turned out in the end, Morarji Desai's political instinct had perhaps been sounder when he said the Janata Party should not show any more interest towards Chikmagalur than they would to any other bye-election. He was for treating it in the normal way, saying the heavens would not fall if she were to return to the Lok Sabha. If the Janata leaders had kept out of the rhetoric and their nervous

[2]Ranajit Roy in *Business Standard*. 3 November 1978.

excitement and just shown Mrs Gandhi as a frightened lady trying to get into the Lok Sabha through a safe back door, they could at least have deprived her of the chance to say that her victory was a vindication of all that she had done during the Emergency.

All the frenzy and excitement that the ruling party and others showed over her candidature only made her more imperious—and testier. When a correspondent asked her if she was going back to Parliament to escape from going into oblivion or to escape the consequences of Shah Commission, she shot back: "Do you think I was in the background all these months? Don't just repeat any and everything that people say."

"If there is any element of surprise about the result," commented a Delhi Editor,[3] "it is the relatively moderate margin of Mrs Gandhi's victory." The victory, came the comment from an American paper, was a "great deal worse than if disgraced Nixon had been reelected to the Congress."[4] The lights were off at 12 Willingdon Crescent when the first results from Chikmagalur started coming in. But the lady of the house went about carrying a flashlight in her hand, a smile on her face. All the heroes of the Emergency were milling around the place: Shukla, Bhinder, Yunus, Dhawan and of course Brahmachari. With victory certain, Mrs Gandhi was going to attend a reception at the Soviet Embassy in honour of the October Revolution. As she was about to drive out, she lost her temper when a man shouted "Jawaharlal Nehru Zindabad" and drove him out of the gate.[5]

Supremely confident that her hour had struck, Mrs Gandhi discarded her *khaddars*, donned heavy silks, got a new hair-do and took off for London. Initially there had been a scramble among the Indian organisations in London to jump on the Indira bandwagon, but gradually a hostile atmosphere had built up. The Friends of India Society International had sent out letters all over England saying that her visit to attend her father's birthday celebration was only an excuse to "re-establish herself with your British politicians...try to project herself as a sinned person rather than a sinner....You should tell her she was an unwanted person." Many enthusiasts had started having second thoughts and some even wondered if she should come

[3]S. M. in Editor's Notebook, the *Indian Express*, 9 November 1978.
[4]*Sun Times*, Chicago.
[5]*The Statesman*, 8 November 1978.

at all. Wouldn't the visit cause an embarrassment to Prime Minister Callaghan? He was already in a minority and there was the possibility that he might have to go to the polls. Surely he wouldn't like to annoy the Indian community. But the Chikmagalur result caused a new spurt of interest in Mrs Gandhi's visit and even James Callaghan felt encouraged to confirm that he would welcome Mrs Gandhi to No. 10 for talks and tea.

At Heathrow, she got the most hostile reception ever accorded abroad to any Indian political leader, reported a correspondent.[6] "Fascist Indira Gandhi," "Dictator Go Back" were the placards amid black flag demonstrators who drowned the slogans of those in her favour. She had been drawn to a ten-minute impromptu press conference at which she had promptly launched her tirade against the Janata Government. This, it was noted, amounted to a virtual violation of the Delhi Magistrate's order which had allowed a passport to be issued to her for ten days on the explicit condition that she would not indulge in any political activity abroad.

Reactions in the British Press that morning had been even more hostile than the protests of Indians. *The Sunday Times* editorial called her "a thoroughly corrupt person and an unwelcome visitor.... Unlike Mrs Gandhi's India this is a free country. Therefore anyone who wants to come here on a visit should be free to do so. This does not mean, however, that Mrs Gandhi should be welcomed, celebrated, honoured or in any way acknowledged by politicians with a claim to represent the people of this country...." Hostile demonstrators and nosy pressmen dogged her wherever she went. Security precautions were the most stringent ever enforced for any visiting politician. The Claridges Hotel where she stayed was virtually blocked by police barricades.

She became testier as the visit progressed. Even those who had watched her Frost interview on the TV did not fail to be shocked by the brazenness of her answers on the Sanjay topic. "I don't know what you people are talking about," she burst out at the Napoleon Room in Cafe Royal where all the world's press had gathered for a reception hosted by the British MP, Michael Foot. "What did Sanjay do? Nothing. It was only in 1975 or '76 that he started taking a little interest. That is all."

On 17 November she had travelled to the picturesque Welsh

[6] V. M. Nair, *The Statesman*, 13 November 1978.

valley to open a spiral steel mill set up by an Indian millionaire, Swaraj Paul, who was also the co-ordinator of Mrs Gandhi's programme in Britain. It was widely rumoured that Mrs Gandhi too had put her money into the mill. An Indian reporter visiting England at that time had followed her to Wales that morning and returned with hilarious tidbits on the sycophancy of some of the British Commoners on the lady's bandwagon. Michael Foot had made one of the most "obnoxious speeches" describing the lady as the "unifier of India" and as a "champion of liberty." It was as sick a speech as she herself made and both were moved to tears at what each had to say about the other. 'You know I was in a hostel when I first went to Oxford, she was saying, 'I was a lonely frightened girl, as frightened as any foreign student can be and then a girl came and knocked at my door and asked if she could come in...Oh, I was so very lonely...' And then she was going about on how Nye Bevan had his great chats with her father and how she herself felt she was half Welsh, how she related to the Welsh people, how concerned she was about the Welsh affairs.... and that was about the time the factory mechanics went into tears. The great Mrs Gandhi had mesmerized the impoverished Welsh audience. Poor Michael Foot was wiping his eyes. The great Nehru connection.... that had done it. "I never saw two politicians so mutually moved as Mrs Gandhi and Foot," said the young reporter.

It was all very moving, but she could hardly have liked the weekly, *Economist*, reminding the people that "she should not be allowed to win the international approval she was seeking," nor the *Sunday Telegraph* advising that "cool politeness is probably the wisest attitude for British public figures to adopt towards the former Indian dictator."

Never a word of remorse or contrition did she ever utter. Nor would she rule out the possibility of seeking, in the event of an electoral victory of the Congress (I) to be Prime Minister again.[7] Personally she had never desired to be Prime Minister again, she told a press conference. But then she had also denied any desire to contest the bye-election to Parliament and she was now back in the Lok Sabha, she said. What if the people were to ask her to take over as Prime Minister again? "I cannot say anything categorically, but I personally would not like to be (Prime Minister again)," she

[7]*The Statesman*, 19 November 1978.

replied. In a letter written in 1965 when she was Information and Broadcasting Minister, she had said: "It may seem strange that a person in politics should be wholly without political ambition but I am afraid that I am that sort of a freak."[8] One year after she wrote this, she was the Prime Minister. But she thought she was 'wholly without political ambition'!

Cheers and jeers greeted the MP from Chikmagalur as she entered the Lok Sabha on 20 November, flanked by Vasant Sathe and C.M. Stephen. "Evil has come back to Parliament" shouted the CPM member Jyotirmoy Bosu and cries of "Hitler" came from the Janata benches, but her lieutenants retorted with "Indira Gandhi ki jai." Watching the scene from the Speaker's Gallery was Devaraj Urs who was already claiming to his friends in the press that it was he who "sent her to Parliament." Stephen dutifully offered his seat to Mrs Gandhi, but she politely declined and took her seat between him and Vasant Sathe, her principal drum-beaters in the House.

She was there for hardly a day when fresh troubles began. The Lok Sabha committee of privileges had held her guilty of serious breach of privilege and contempt of the House and left it to the "collective wisdom of the House to award such punishment as it may deem fit." The question of privilege had been raised by Madhu Limaye and Kanwar Lal Gupta, both Janata members, and referred to the privileges committee on 18 November 1977. She had been accused of obstruction, intimidation, harassment and institution of false cases against certain officials who were collecting information for answer, to a question on Maruti Limited for the Fifth Lok Sabha. The committee, said its report, had come to the "inescapable conclusion" that Mrs Gandhi had misused her office of Prime Minister with an intention 'to protect the interest of the Maruti Limited controlled and managed by her son." It had passed similar verdict against her former additional private secretary, R.K. Dhawan, and D. Sen, former Director of the Central Bureau of Investigation.

When it came to deciding the course of action against Mrs Gandhi, nearly all the Parties were sharply divided. The Janata Party itself was split up among the hawks and the doves. While both

[8]Quoted in Nayantara Sehgal's *Indira Gandhi's Emergence and Style.*

Morarji Desai and Charan Singh were for once united on the need for 'stern action', Atal Behari Vajpayee suggested that a 'reprimand' would be enough, and even L.K. Advani was initially in favour of a soft line until he fell behind Desai. The CPM made its stand clear through its Politbureau resolution: "...There has been a lot of dithering and softness when hard political decisions had to be taken. In such a situation to strike heroic and militant poses on the privilege issue and demand extreme action will be counter-productive in the struggle against authoritarianism and give an excuse to opponents to appear as martyrs and claim the sympathy of the people." It was sensible, but a non-performing Government which had nothing positive to show for itself could not but strike a heroic pose when it got an easy chance to do so. Mrs Gaudhi was a sitting duck for them, and the hawks were determined to get her no matter what the political advantage it would give the lady. For once Mrs Gandhi's words struck sympathetic chords throughout the country when she told the Lok Sabha: "The failures of this Government are leading to its isolation from people everywhere. The ineptitude of this Government has destroyed the cohesiveness of the administration and created a situation of uncertainty and insecurity. If this situation is not reversed it will provide fertile soil for the growth of fascism."

Growth of fascism, symbolized by Mrs Gandhi herself, was what the Government helped by deciding to expel her from the House. Hardly a parliamentarian to have put the Yamuna on fire, she could have been contained by letting her be in the House. By throwing her out she was being provoked to seek power outside the system— a game she excelled at.

The expelled MP from Chikmagalur would not leave the House without extracting the maximum mileage out of the show. For three hours after the Lok Sabha had decided to expel her and send her to jail, she had refused to budge from the House and during that time she turned the House into a comic opera with shouting and singing and kissing in full view of a jampacked press gallery. The moment the Speaker adjourned the House—at 5.05 p.m. on 19 December— all her men and women rushed to her. There she was in her seat, now dictating a statement to the reporters and now kissing and hugging her daughters-in-law who had arrived for the show. "Since I am in the custody of the House, I should be taken to prison from the House itself." Her histrionics and the poses she struck were

reminiscent of that other day in October 1977 when she was first
arrested. It was only around 9 p.m. that the security chief of Parliament brought the Speaker's formal warrant and she got up to go.
There had been enough time once again to collect the crowds and
the drum-beaters for a triumphant journey to Tihar. "Every step the
Government has taken against me helped me," she had boasted to
reporters in London. And indeed they had.

VII

LOSS OF KARNATAKA

Devaraj Urs has an uncanny similarity to Lalit Narayan Mishra, that other lieutenant of Mrs Gandhi whose life was cut short all too suddenly in January 1975. Political non-entities until 1969, both shot up fast, one in Delhi, the other in Karnataka. Urs became as great a money spinner as L.N. Mishra was. Both were big spenders, obsessed with the astral world, and easy prey to all manner of tantriks and soothsayers. Like Mishra, Urs had started as a simple, homely man, and the lifestyles of both changed dramatically. Their appetite for the good things of life was amazing, though Mishra never took to Dunhills or Napoleon brandy. Charming and open-hearted men, they had shared a flair for the niceties of political intrigue, and for long enjoyed the lady's implicit trust. There were many other things in common between the two, including nagging wives at home, but then there was a very basic difference. Both soared high, but while Mishra did so on a string whose other end was held by Mrs Gandhi, Urs had stuck roots in the ground which even she found hard to uproot.

Like Mishra, Urs too was nothing if not a creation of Mrs Gandhi. Though he had been a member of the Karnataka Assembly ever since 1952, and served as a Minister for Sericulture under Nijalingappa, it was only after the Congress split of 1969 that his rise began. Those were the days when Karnataka was in the vice-like grip of the two major castes of the State, the Lingayats and the Vokkaligas. Politics, administration, education, in fact no sphere of life was free from their stranglehold. Nobody could even imagine that a man belonging to another community could become a force in the State, far less the Chief Minister. When the split came most of the power-ful Lingayats and Vokkaligas were ranged on the other side. Mrs Gandhi calculated that she could not build her strength in the State without striking at the two major castes. For this she chose Devaraj Urs.

Urs belonged to the Ursu community whose number did not go beyond ten thousand or so—just about 0.5 per cent of the State's population. It had seemed a strange choice to many, especially because the party had to be built up from a scratch. But Urs, whom she made the ad hoc president of the new party, plunged into the task with indomitable zeal. He rented a small house for the party office and when faced with shortage of space he put up some tents in the compound. Often there was not enough fund even for coffee at press conferences. He had some cows which he and his wife looked after, and he supplemented his meagre income by selling some of the milk. By then his younger brother, Kempraj Urs had become a film celebrity in Madras. In one of his moments of financial stress, Devaraj decided to go and seek help from his brother. "Why did you have to join politics?" Kempraj had told him contemptuously and shut the door in his face. Undeterred, Devaraj had returned to his work of organising the new Congress.

It was Mrs Gandhi's sweeping victory in the 1971 Lok Sabha elections that set the pace for new politics in Karnataka. All the Syndicate bosses were swept away and people looked up to the new party for a change. As the State party chief, Urs was given almost a free hand to choose the candidates for the 1972 Assembly elections and he did it with a sure eye to the future. He gave full play to his concept of "distributive justice," which meant a far greater share of the party tickets to the backwards and the minorities. The dominating class and caste were synonymous and Urs was determined to break this hegemony. He was aware that the cumulative outcome of the measures he had in mind would mean a class war, and was quite prepared to sow its seeds. He openly accused the majority castes of being the blood-suckers of society. "I tried to mobilize and educate the other classes, or castes, if you like, and I succeeded. I won 165 of the 216 Assembly seats. After that no permutation or combination could work against me."[1]

But though his party had won a majority in the Assembly, Urs himself had not contested, for the first time since 1952. Some of his antagonists in the party had persuaded Mrs Gandhi to agree that the candidates for the Assembly seats should first resign from party positions. Urs had preferred to keep his party post, and so it appeared he was nowhere in the race for chief ministership. There were at least two stalwart Lingayat leaders of the party who had been elected—Chammabasappa and Sidhaveerappa—and most people thought one of the two would emerge as the legislature party leader. How could the great Lingayats be ignored ?

Sure enough, Sidhaveerappa announced his candidature. But so did Devaraj Urs. Many laughed at him. What cheek to contest Sidhaveerappa, they said. Umashankar Dixit flew down from Delhi as Mrs Gandhi's emissary to conduct the election of leader. Dixit called an informal meeting of the party's new MLAs to know their mind, and it turned out that a big majority wanted Urs. By the time the legislators formally met at the Vidhan Soudha, the result seemed to be a foregone conclusion, but Sidhaveerappa was not prepared to give up so easily. There must have been some mistake somewhere, he was certain. How could Mrs Gandhi want a non-entity, and a non-Lingayat, non-Vokkaliga at that, to be the Chief Minister ? Impossible. He got up to say that no matter what the MLAs thought, they must first get the clearance from Mrs Gandhi, the "Supreme Leader." Dixit, himself a mere creature of Mrs Gandhi, could not say no. The meeting was adjourned and Dixit drove to the Raj Bhawan to talk to Mrs Gandhi on the phone. When the legislators reassembled that afternoon, Dixit announced that Mrs Gandhi wanted Devaraj Urs.

Why had Mrs Gandhi chosen him ? To this day nobody seems to know for sure. Perhaps she thought he would be the right instrument for breaking the power of the Vokkaligas and the Lingayats. Or maybe she chose him for the very reason that the Syndicate bosses had once chosen her to be Prime Minister—that she would remain a *gungi gudia* in their hands. But if that was the reason, Mrs Gandhi had made as great a mistake as Kamaraj and other Syndicate bosess.

[1]Devaraj Urs in an interview with the author in early 1978.

Urs, however, was not in all that hurry. An avid reader of Kautilya's *Arthashastra*, his sense of timing was as uncanny as Mrs Gandhi's. 'Step by step' has been his rule—one enemy at a time. The first enemy to be fought was the ruling caste combine and in this he had all the support of Mrs Gandhi. One of the most powerful means he chose to break the backbone of the ruling castes in the rural areas was his debt relief measures, which he implemented with great gusto. Land legislation in Karnataka became the most progressive in the country. In every taluka of the State, Urs set up five-man land tribunals and made it obligatory for one of the members to be a Harijan. Representatives of the minorities and the backward castes were nominated liberally to these tribunals, whose decisions were not subject to appeal, except through writ petitions in the High Court. Urs said he had done this to avoid legal wrangles and delays, and when nearly 15,000 writ petitions against the decisions of the land tribunals piled up in the High Court, he took the stand that even the judiciary in the country was not free from corruption, a stand which further enhanced his grass-root popularity.

His work towards the abolition of bonded labour and the distribution of house sites to the landless villagers became a model of radical social change for other parts of the country. During the seven years of his chief ministership, occupancy rights had been given to over two and a half lakh tenants spread over an area of more than ten lakh acres and more than eight lakh house sites were distributed. Urs also set about reorganising the cooperative societies which had been the exclusive preserve of the ruling castes, and when his measure was struck down by the High Court, he rose once again in the eyes of the common people.

The common people figured high in his scheme of things, but he was too pragmatic to stop at that. He was all the time creating his own power bases, tapping the sources for his political war chest. Too practical not to know that power politics could not be played without money, he had no compunctions about raising funds, no matter how. In his earlier days as Chief Minister one of his financiers was K.K. Murthy, a former kerosene dealer who had been a confidant of Nijalingappa. Urs made Murthy chairman of the Karnataka Film Development Corporation to the mutual benefit of both. But Urs was soon on to bigger fish. There was H.R. Basavaraj, one of the biggest excise contractors of the South.

Mrs Indira Gandhi
setting off to meet
Vinoba Bhave at
Punar Ashram

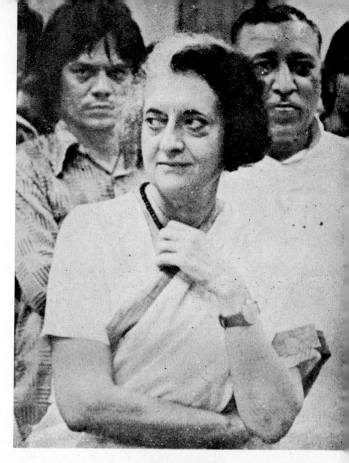

Arguing with police-
men before being
arrested in October
1977   ↓

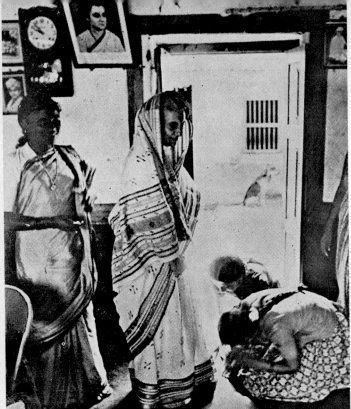

Her devotees at her feet

The way her supporters campaigned for her

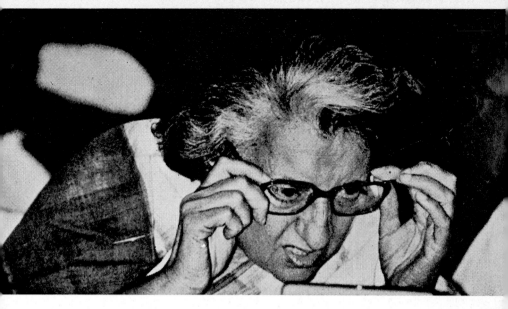

Looking at the election results from Chickmagalur

At the "Comeback" dinner at Karnataka Bhawan

Addressing the May 6th rally

Mrs Gandhi starts on her journey

Sanjay Gandhi with Bansi Lal and
N. D. Tewari

Dhirendra Brahmachari

Morarji Desai walking out of Rashtrapati Bhawan after submitting his resignation to the President

Mrs Gandhi with Charan Singh and Raj Narain

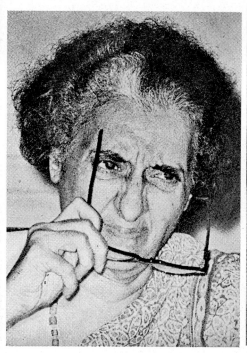
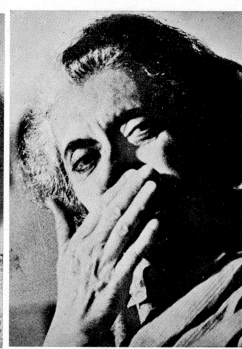

In her various moods

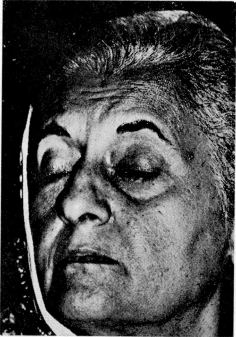

Apart from having his own distillery, he also owned a theatre and what was more important, a newspaper which could be used for projecting the leader's image. So fruitful was the association for both that Basavaraj was awarded a seat in the Rajya Sabha. During the second Congress split, when Yashpal Kapoor was pressing Urs for money to keep the *National Herald* going, it was through Basavaraj that a good part of the Rs 52 lakhs came. In return, Basavaraj was put on the board of directors of Nehru's newspaper. There was other financiers, among them the Khodays, another big wine merchants and distillery-owners, and industrialist Panduranga Setty, who was to figure prominently in the Grover Commission report which indicted Urs and some of his Cabinet colleagues. A piece of prize land which had been set aside for a stadium in Bangalore was given away to Setty at throwaway price. Yet another "banker" of the Chief Minister was a building contractor who had lately built a posh multi-storied hotel close to Balabrooie, the official residence of Urs, and there were critics who said Urs himself had substantial business interests in the venture. He certainly had several special suites set apart in the hotel for his special guests, just as L.N. Mishra used to have in some of the hotels of Delhi.

Urs, however, was not the man to make any bones about his closeness to contractors and business tycoons. So what if they were close to him? Had that made any difference to his concern for the poor? He would often challenge any detractor to show him one instance where his connections with businessmen had biased his actions. Urs is deeply religious, deeply superstitious, but he is certainly not a purist. Indeed, he does not give a damn about morality and so forth. In his close circles, he even revels in being "unethical." Everything about him is compartmentalised, as it were. Religion and superstition in its own place, politics in its own, and so too his personal life. In spite of his great obsession with holy men and the almost daily *yajnas* that go on for him, Urs is completely secular and modern in his outlook. A queer fish, just the sort to succeed in the murky waters of Indian politics.

Money and Mrs Gandhi had been important in the building up of his political strength. But there was much more to it. No other Chief Minister in the country had been as generous as Urs in distributing favours of all sorts. In political favours, he simply excelled. In the sheer number of Corporations and Boards he created, he left Devi Lal and such other Chief Ministers far behind. By the end of 1978, there were about 75 of them going in Karnataka, three for forests, three for agriculture, three for industries. There was the Finance Corporation for Backward Classes and yet another for the Scheduled Castes and Tribes. You could name almost anything and there was a Board or a Corporation to look after it. Seventy-five of them meant 75 chairmen, each with a free house and a free car and so many other perks to go with the job. Only with a little bit of intelligence a chairman of one of these boards could end up with a neat pile of ten to fifteen lakhs of rupees at the end of his term. Urs had found other ways of combining social service with political and personal gains. He set up district level recruitment committees all over the State and nominated a lot of non-officials to them. Thereby he not only created a body of people loyal to him but also opened up more avenues for appointments of local people. And if his critics could be believed, these committees even functioned as local-level "collection agencies." Perhaps what irked the Lingayats and the Vokkaligas most was that this was one of the surest ways of breaking the age-old hegemony of the ruling coteries in the State.

Within years Urs had become the most powerful Chief Minister in the country. Even after his dismissal from office, when he was facing challenges from all sides, he was all too conscious of his basic strength. Talking to me at that time, away in the luxury of his favourite cottage in the Palace grounds which many described as his "fun place," he had said: "My biggest asset is that I am Urs." Mixed with the aroma of Dunhill tobacco was that of the rich-brewed coffee that the liveried bearers brought in every half hour.

For his swearing-in as the Chief Minister in 1972, Urs had turned up in a worn-out kurta. Right until the early fifties, he had often tilled his own land—about ten or twelve acres in his little village of Kallahalli in Mysore district. At his first press conference as the Chief Minister, Urs had handed around Panama cigarettes to the correspondents. That was what he himself smoked in those days.

"You are still smoking Panamas!" a correspondent had joked, to which Urs had said: "What do you mean? Devaraj will never change. Panama is my brand and so it will remain." Months later came his second or third press conference and out came packets

of 555. From that day he never went below India Kings. He took
to pipe-smoking in a big way and developed a special taste for
Napoleon brandy. Soon he had acquired the choicest array of
briar pipes, nearly 75 of them, and in his leisure hours he would
often browse through Dunhill's *Pipe Book*. Despite all his predi-
lections for sadhus and saints he had acquired a convincing veneer
of sophistication—a trait that gives great mileage to politicians in
this country. You could hear the scented and bejewelled ladies in
the 5-star hotels cooing over Mrs Gandhi just because she was "oh
so sophisticated!". Great asset, indeed. So is hypocrisy, but Urs
did not mind telling friends that "one of the advantages of being
a Chief Minister is that people keep you supplied with imported
stuff."

Urs had come a long way from the political non-entity he had
been in 1969. He owed a great deal to Mrs Gandhi, and he was
willing to acknowledge it. "I would be less than fair," he said
after his complete break with her in June 1979, "if I don't even
at this moment express my thanks and regards to Srimati Indira
Gandhi, with whom I have shared many political experiences
since 1969. As she gave me her support and co-operation during
this period, so also did I during her hours of trial and need...."

A break between them was inevitable in the very nature of
things. Urs was far too ambitious and much too conscious of his
great potential to go on playing a second fiddle to her, and he
certainly wouldn't do it to the young upstart who seemed to lead
her by the nose. Urs was not the type to remain content with being
a Zail Singh or a Jagannath Mishra or a Narayan Dutt Tewari. Mrs
Gandhi's debacle of 1977 had given him second thoughts about
the lady. She had gone down in his estimation, and privately he
would often express his horror at the strange power that Sanjay
Gandhi seemed to have over his mother. The trouble with Mrs
Gandhi, he would say, was that she was surrounded by half a
dozen sycophants who went to her morning, afternoon, evening
and night and fed her with all kinds of nonsense.

Even at a more ideological level, he had a bone to pick with
her. He thought she had lost the North because of her worthless
chief ministers. They had failed to implement the party programme; they had wanted to please both the rich and the poor
and had fallen between two stools. All his blasphemous remarks
were dutifully carried to Delhi by the Sanjay zealots, Gundu Rao,

F.M. Khan and Jaffer Sharief. These men never stopped breathing down Urs' neck. They expected him to be one of them and every time Urs showed his guts they jetted to Delhi with their tales of "treachery". The seeds of suspicion had taken roots by mid-78. By then Urs had sensed the efforts that were on to cut him down to size. He had little doubt that the talks about relieving him from the presidentship of the State party would only be a prelude to his ouster from chief ministership.

Chikmagalur election was the watershed in the relations between Urs and Mrs Gandhi. Till then they had hung on together because each needed the other. In the words of a perceptive Bangalore journalist, Mrs Gandhi had wanted his credibility, and Urs her charisma. But the Chikmagalur elections had suddenly exposed the hollowness of Mrs Gandhi's charisma. He knew better than anyone else what her fate would have been if he hadn't done what he did during the last few days of the campaign. A reporter who had closely followed the campaign described to me how wads of currency notes were distributed among the Kurubas (shepherds). It was largely because of Urs that the Lingayat votes in Tarikere, Birur and Kadur went over to Mrs Gandhi. "I don't want to tell you what all I did," Urs told several journalists. "Do you call this a victory? Where is her charisma? Tell me."

But he knew it was not time yet to break. He must hold on till he found another anchor. Being one of the principal pillars of the Congress (I) he was under increasing attack from the Janata Government. In January 1979, the Union Cabinet decided on a follow-up action on the first report of the Grover Commission which had upheld four of the seven charges against Urs. Most important were the charges of favouritism in appointing his brother, Kempraj Urs, as Director of the Karnataka Film Development Corporation, and nepotism in granting land to his son-in-law, M.D. Nataraj in violation of the rules. By the time Devaraj Urs had become the Chief Minister, the fortunes of his younger brother had dipped low and he had gone over to Bangalore to seek his brother's help. The scales had turned. Kempraj, however, managed to worm his way into the affections of his brother and the story went that it was actually Kempraj's wife who had managed to bring about a reconciliation between the brothers. According to a Bangalore journalist[2] who did a book on Devaraj Urs, the sister-in-law, Lalitha, got a chance to nurse the ailing Chief Minister and she did such a good job of it that he was charmed into forgiving the past insolence of his younger brother. Be that as it may, Kempraj had not only been made the Director of the KFDC, but had also become one of the important political fixtures in the State, quite an eyesore for the antagonists of Urs. And now even the Grover Commission had established the favouritism charge against Urs.

Though the State Government itself had the authority to register regular cases for investigation on the basis of the Grover Commission report, Urs was nonetheless rattled. Even though prosecution was out of the question, Urs being the Chief Minister himself, the report was a handle in the hands of his political foes in the State. It was what made him stick to Mrs Gandhi longer than he would otherwise have. He made repeated public statements accusing the Janata Party of adopting a policy of persecution against him and Mrs Gandhi, whose farm house had been raided just about that time. It was very curious, Urs said, that Prime Minister Desai had not agreed to probe the charges against Kanti Desai on the ground that Mrs Gandhi had cleared them, and yet he had appointed the Grover Commission against him even though the charges had been cleared by Mrs Gandhi. "Why this political vendetta?" he asked.[3]

Both Mrs Gandhi and Devaraj Urs were looking around for possible ways of acquiring more strength to fight the onslaughts from the Janata Government. Soon after the Chikmagalur victory of Mrs Gandhi, a good part of the Congress was almost itching to jump on to the Indira band wagon. "The only way, they imagine, they can continue to display that label and enjoy the privileges of office again is to fall at Mrs Gandhi's feet,"[4] said one political commentator. In Parliament, leaders of the Congress (I) were already counting the heads which would jump over to their side. They even talked about their negotiations with a "majority group" in the Janata Party which was "poised" to join hands with them. The obvious reference was to Charan Singh and his followers. From the Tihar Jail the lady had sent a large birthday bouquet along with a charming message straight to the Kisan rally and the mammoth Jat

[2]I.K. Jagirdar in *Arsu Adalitaranga* : *Chronicle of Karnataka Political Developments in the seventies.*
[3]*The Times of India*, 13 February 1978.
[4]Ranajit Roy in *Business Standard*, 10 November 1978.

brotherhood of Charan Singh had gone wild with joy at the news. Their leader had been treated so shabbily by Morarji and his Jan Sangh supporters that a tie-up with Indira Gandhi had seemed to them the only right step to take. But it was just this fear which made the Janata leaders to insist on fresh negotiations between Desai and Charan Singh. Before the lady could make any fresh overtures to Charan Singh, he had already crawled back to a chair in the Janata Government, this time as Deputy Prime Minister with Finance portfolio.

With that front closed for the moment, Mrs Gandhi and Devaraj Urs began trying out other possible alignments. Congress President Swaran Singh would have jumped over without the asking but for the fact that Y.B. Chavan was holding him hard. Even so, Swaran Singh rushed over to her place for a late night meeting on 26 February, the very day that Sanjay was convicted, and even signed a joint statement saying that steps to unite the two parties were on. "We hope nothing would be done to hamper the process," the statement said.[5] Next morning, Swaran Singh held out the hope that unity would be achieved "within three weeks." The anti-unity camp in the Congress was, however, aware of the objectives of Mrs Gandhi: to wreck the Congress, destroy the political careers of Y.B. Chavan and his followers, and absorb as many of the Congress MPs as possible. They knew that the main factors that were prompting Mrs Gandhi to rush through unity were the conviction of Sanjay Gandhi and the Special Courts. Some of these members, including Dev Kant Barooah, K.P. Unnikrishnan, Mrs Ambika Soni, Saugata Roy and Dada Rupwate, met at the residence of Dinesh Goswami and proclaimed that the Indira-Swaran Singh joint statement was a "camouflage" to entrap Congressmen into a position where they could be used by Mrs Gandhi for her "selfish motives." They wanted the unity talks to be stopped at once. The resistance to unity was strong precisely in areas where the Congress was still a force: Maharashtra, Gujarat, Assam and Kerala. At one stage Urs arranged a meeting between Indira Gandhi and Rajni Patel, Vasantdada Patil and N.M. Tidke, but it proved no good. She started off by complaining that the Congress MPs were supporting the bill on Special Courts. The other side talked in a round-about manner about ensuring "inner party democracy" and

[5]*The Times of India*, 27 February 1979.

non-interference by the Sanjay caucus, a point on which she was most touchy. The anti-unity group grew bolder with the defeat of Mrs Gandhi's party in Samastipur, Fatehpur and other bye-elections to the Lok Sabha. These had taken much of the wind out of Mrs Gandhi's sails, and suddenly she was facing rough weather inside her own party in various states. In Tamilnadu, some of the prominent members of her party had boycotted one of her meetings and dissidence was suddenly mounting in West Bengal against the strong-arm methods of the Sanjay hoodlums who had been foisted on the State party.

When Mrs Gandhi visited Calcutta in early March, an ugly factional violence broke out right at the reception arranged for her. Back in her hotel she gave a dressing down to some of the members of the State party: "If some people do not like Sanjay Gandhi's association with the organisation, they are free to quit the party." She made it absolutely clear that the Sanjay question was not negotiable. Nor would she harbour any complaints against the Sanjay crony, Kamal Nath, who was virtually dictating to the organisation. "Is it not that there is a divided loyalty at some level of the party?" she asked imperiously. She couldn't understand people wanting to be loyal to her and not to Sanjay. That clearly was an anathema to her.

The Calcutta posture of Mrs Gandhi further hardened the attitude of the anti-unity group. "No surrender" was their slogan now. Sharad Pawar, with the blessings of Y.B. Chavan, launched a full-scale campaign against the unity move, and at last on 12 March the Congress finally declared that the chapter was over: on more unity talks. "This is one of my happiest birthdays," a beaming Chavan had told Swaran Singh when he went to wish him happy returns of the day. The 66-year-old Maratha from Satara was bubbling with joy, as he told reporters, "The inevitable has happened. Mrs Gandhi did not want honourable colleagues but prisoners of surrender." Antony looked jubilant and Barooah was bursting with a sense of *deja vu* : "What I have been saying for one year has happened. I don't walk with my feet on my head."

It was over as far as Indira Gandhi and the Congress was concerned, but not for Devaraj Urs. Far from it. Two days after the matter was finally closed, he told reporters in Bangalore that he would be making another effort for unity and that Mrs Gandhi was not against unity. Nor did Sanjay Gandhi have anything to do with the unity— "he is not a factor at all." By that time, Urs was already on to his own plans: realignment *sans* Mrs Gandhi. What had made him desperate was the submission of the final report of the Grover Commission on 17 March. He had to find support outside the Congress (I), and this could not be done with the liability of Mrs Gandhi and her son. Even when he was totally committed to her, he had not given up any of his old contacts with his friends in other parties, whether it was Antony in Kerala or Sharad Pawar and Rajni Patel in Bombay or Chandra Shekhar in Delhi. He now set out to explore new possibilities on his own.

Goenka's penthouse in the Express Towers, Bombay, is quite a rendezvous of politicians, businessmen and journalists. It was there that Devaraj Urs had an important meeting with Chandra Shekhar, George Fernandes, Sharad Pawar and Rajni Patel. Both Chandra Shekhar and George were sick of the old fuddy-duddies of the Janata Party, as so many others were, but they could hardly see a way out. Much as everybody felt that the Janata Party could not go on in the manner it was, nobody knew how or when it would break. At this meeting, however, they got down to discussing the possibility of former Congressmen, wherever they were, coming together—minus Mrs Gandhi, of course. On the Janata front, Chandra Shekhar and Fernandes were agreed that they would have to eventually isolate Morarji Desai and perhaps later the Jan Sangh. None of them really minded the Jan Sangh being there, not even Urs. Chandra Shekhar lost no time in letting his views go out to the press. He told a news agency that he was for an accord with the anti-Indira faction of the Congress and that a realignment was desirable. As for the anti-RSS campaign, he said "it is politics." Within a few days Y.B. Chavan was in Bombay, agreeing with Chandra Shekhar's views when they met at a dinner. Chavan told Chandra Shekhar that there could certainly be co-operation between the Janata Party and the anti-Indira group in the Congress.

Urs had already established his pipeline with Charan Singh, mainly through his "adopted daughter," a young IFS officer posted in Delhi, who almost acted as his political liaison chief. Urs had even opened a secret dialogue with Jagjivan Ram, and had started trying to convince him that time was after all running out for

Charan Singh, and after him Ram would of course be the natural leader.

Urs was quite aware that nothing was going to come off immediately. He was only probing all sorts of possibilities, and in the process he was fairly assured that he need not worry too much about the Grover Commission report. There were plenty of friends all around to come to his aid, more so if he were to cut Mrs Gandhi off. That was what he would do next. He calculated each and every move and decided he would not hurry. Nor would he give the impression that it was he who wanted a break. Slowly does it, step by step.

He fired the first shot at the AICC (I) meeting on 21 April 1979. "Let people stop going surreptitiously to Mr Sanjay Gandhi," he said, "else I will expose such people." Cleverly he added, "Any efforts to bring about a rift between me and Mrs Gandhi on this issue is not going to help either the party or the country . . . I believe in the policies and programmes of the Congress and in the leadership of Mrs Gandhi . . . but don't mistake me for a sycophant . . . ."

Urs knew it was a deliberate challenge flung in Mrs Gandhi's face. He had meant it to be that. The shots went home. She made no secret of her annoyance over Urs' remarks on Sanjay. After Urs had finished his speech and sat down, she was seen talking to him animatedly. Urs stood up and left with a "namaste."

The attack on Sanjay was taken up by Mrs Tarkeshwari Sinha with even greater vehemence. "Some people have formed a saturn's ring round you," she told Mrs Gandhi. "*Aapke aur aapke ladke ke naam par dukan lagate hain* (they are trading in your name and in the name of your son)."

Mrs Gandhi could not take it. She flared up and said the meeting had been convened to discuss issues, not personalities. "I am not going to allow it," Mrs Sinha was shouted down by the party hounds, some of them even calling her names. Mrs Sinha flung her papers and declared she was walking out in protest. Outside, she said : "We are ready to accept Mrs Gandhi as our leader but not her dogs."

The crunch came in late April when Urs virtually refused to join Sanjay Gandhi in his plan to take the battle against the Janata

Party to the streets. Sanjay's men in Karnataka were itching to bring the whole State, as it were, to the streets of Delhi for the 16 May rally against the Special Courts. But they could hardly manage that without official help. Instead of helping, Urs decided to clip their wings. At a meeting of the Karnataka Pradesh Congress(I) Committee, he got a resolution passed banning all ministers and party legislators from participating in the rally. "Yes, we have a right to protest," he told reporters, "but it must be through public meetings and things of that sort. No violence, if we indulge in violence, we shall be going against our own creed."[6] His argument was simple : what if there was a law and order problem and the ministers and legislators got arrested ? An argument that anybody but Mrs Gandhi and her son could understand. As for anti-Special Court rallies in Karnataka, Urs made it plain that he would tolerate them only as long as they were within constitutional limits. "If the agitators exceed the limit I will put them behind the bars," he declared.

Addressing a convention of Congressmen at Ahmedabad on 6 May, Urs said "personalities are no doubt important, but the party's policies and programmes are more important than personalities." He was clearly becoming more and more defiant.

On 8 May, Jaffer Sharief returned to Bangalore from Delhi and in a chat with reporters said he was going to demand that Urs must relinquish the PCC presidentship. When no paper took note of it, Sharief sent off a telegram next morning to Mrs Gandhi pressing that Urs should be relieved of his post. He passed on copies of the telegram to the newspaper offices to ensure publication. To anybody familiar with the way Mrs Gandhi's party worked, it was clear that Sharief was merely acting at the behest of the lady — or of Sanjay, which was really the same thing.

A day later Mrs Gandhi herself arrived in Bangalore en route to Chikmagalur for the marriage of an MLA's daughter. She spent the whole day in the city, but the Chief Minister was away at Kudremukh along with the Steel Minister, Biju Patnaik. That evening nearly half a dozen met her. At the very mention of Urs, she flared up: "He is trying to hobnob with people who want to kill me. . . ." She had kept herself informed about all the movements of Urs, his meetings with the Janata Party leaders in Bombay, his

[6]*The Times of India*, 27 April 1979.

dinner with Chandra Shekhar and Fernandes in Delhi, his talks with other leaders of the party. "I won't tolerate saboteurs any more," she fumed. One of the party's former MLAs, a Muslim from Raichur district, told her he had been defeated in the last Assembly elections by a margin of merely two or three hundred votes and if only she had visited the constituency he would surely have won. She flared up again: "Why should I have gone to your constituency ? Your Chief Minister says even a girl could have won from Chikmagalur with him there. You should have taken Urs to your constituency, not me !" It was actually Acharya Kripalani who had made the comment; Urs had only been indiscreet enough to repeat it during one of his repartees with the Opposition leader in the Assembly. Even so, one of the Delhi papers had published the remark prominently and Mrs Gandhi's attention was promptly drawn towards it.

Even before leaving for Bangalore, Mrs Gandhi had wired instructions for a PCC meeting to be held on 11 May. She had wanted to settle the issue of presidentship finally. But Urs' men had already organised a gate-crash at the meeting, so that when Mrs Gandhi and Urs arrived at the Palace grounds they found it was more a public gathering than a meeting of the PCC. She was visibly angry but could do nothing. Urs, speaking first, announced that he would soon step down from the PCC presidentship, but made it clear that the new chief would be elected by the KPCC members. When Mrs Gandhi got up to speak, she could hardly contain her rage. She began with a long harangue against the 'inaction' of the PCC. It did nothing, she said, when the Shah Commission had its session in Bangalore. It had been left to a band of Youth Congress boys to demonstrate against the Commission. Nobody had even mentioned Sanjay and yet she was defending him : "Some people come and tell me that I should ask Sanjay to keep off politics for at least one year (a reference to Urs). Why should I do it ? The Congress is not willing to stand by him, he is being harassed and hounded by the Janata Party. Who am I to stop him from doing something ? And why should I prevent him ?"

At a press conference that afternoon, the inevitable question about the PCC presidentship cropped up again. Had the controversy ended with Urs' office ? "The issue will have to be discussed further in Delhi," she said.

By the time she visited Bangalore again, on 3 June, the rift was almost complete. In between had come the set-back on Thanjavur, and she had no doubt Urs had played a "diabolical" rule in persuading M.G. Ramachandran to withdraw his promised support to her. Even so, when reporters met her at the Mangalore airport that morning she told them irascibly that her differences with Urs were being blown out of proportion. She had proceeded to Chikmagalur to attend the marriage of another MLA's daughter. Urs was also to go to the marriage, but he decided he would go for the evening reception rather than the ceremony which was in the morning. Having blessed the new couple, Mrs Gandhi left for Bangalore by car around 1.30 p.m. Urs left Bangalore, also by road, about two hours later. Now, there are two roads connecting Bangalore and Chikmagalur, one via Hassan and the other via Arsikere. Before starting, the Chief Minister had received official information that Mrs Gandhi was coming to Bangalore via Arsikere, the somewhat shorter and more usual route.

"Which way will you be going?" asked a companion hesitantly as the car sped out of his residence. "Via Hassan, of course," Urs replied nonchalantly, chewing his pipe, and his companion did not miss the naughty smile. "I don't want to bump into her," Urs added, making his intention more explicit. It was literally a parting of ways between Urs and Mrs Gandhi, after almost ten years of close association. "She'll wring my neck or I'll wring hers," Urs said his teeth clamping on his pipe-stem. He seemed to be ruminating, speaking more to himself than to the person beside him. "She doesn't know the new tricks. . . she hasn't met another politician like me. . . . Only I can teach her a lesson. I know exactly what she is going to do, I know her moves and I have my countermoves. . . ."

And so it seemed right to the day when the final break came on 21 June, when Urs sent his famous reply to the show-cause notice she had sent him. "You have completely forgotten," he wrote, "that while dealing with us you were not dealing with your domestic servants or satraps. Instead you were dealing with an elected body and its duly elected office-bearers. We refuse to be treated as bonded labour and juniors and subordinates. . . ." A few days later, he was expelled from the Congress (I) and he floated the Karnataka Congress.

Suddenly the lady was in straits. The expected had not happened. The visions of Urs' supporters deserting him like rats on board a sinking ship had proved a chimera. The Sanjay men in Karnataka had counted on her action forcing a mid-term poll in the State in which case her charisma with the voters would bring all Urs' men scampering to her feet. Nothing happened. Not even Yashpal Kapoor, the great toppler of governments, installed with a fat purse in a Bangalore hotel room, could make any headway. The lady had lost Karnataka.

VIII

THE JANATA DEBACLE

A variety of factors brought about the fall of the Janata Government—the overweening ambition of Chaudhuri Charan Singh to become the Prime Minister, the destructive culture of the Lohiaites, the fears and anxieties of the industrialists and business houses, the subtle machinations of the Russian lobby in India, the desperate manoeuvres of Mrs Gandhi and her son to escape the consequences of the Emergency, and last but not least the utter failure of the Janata Government to come to grips with the task of governing the country.

If the Janata Party had any political culture at all it was a polyglot culture, a queer confluence of various political streams. There was the culture of the Jan Sangh, rooted in the ethos of its mother organisation, the RSS, with all its emphasis on monolithic discipline, its unquestioning devotion to the dictates from above. There was the culture of the last remnants of the pre-Independence Congress which had been completely swamped after the emergence of Mrs Gandhi by the catch-as-catch-can Congressmen. They were the power-hungry generation in the Congress, symbolized by the lady. To the Janata Party had returned the moth-eaten old Congressmen, often described as "obscurantists" who had been thrown on the dustheap by the tide of Mrs Gandhi's so-called progressivism. Epitomizing the old Congressmen was the 83-year-old Morarji Desai with his Charkha and urine therapy and his communion with gods, a bizarre character straight out of some old curiosity shop, as it were. But with all his obscurantism and his crabby manners, he still had some vestiges of the old world norms, the quality to break but not bend. In another rush had come some of the power-crazy operators and tuft-hunters of Mrs Gandhi's Congress, people like Biju Patnaik, H.N. Bahuguna, Nandini Satpathy, and of course Babu Jagjivan Ram, a huge mass of filth who personified all the darkest elements that had crept into the Congress after Independence, a darkness which could hardly be redeemed by his well-advertised adroitness as an administrator. There were also some representing a minor sub-culture of the Congress, like Chandra Shekhar, who had for years been with Mrs Gandhi and yet not quite with her, a Hamletian character whose flesh was willing but spirit was not. Nurtured in the school of Acharya Narendra Dev, he had remained something of an 'outsider', which turned out to be his strength, and the more his radical dissidentism was projected the more it became an article of faith with him. And then there were the Socialists, or what was left of them. The socialist movement had undergone a long period of fission and fusion, it had broken up at least half a dozen times, and there were two distinct strains of Socialists who came into the Janata Party. There were the PSP-ites like S.M. Joshi, N.G. Goray and Madhu Dandavate and those belonging to a distinctly different group of fauna—Raj Narain, Madhu Limaye, George Fernandes and others. While Raj Narain had inherited everything that was rough and crude in Lohia and magnified it hundredfold by his own crudeness, he had imbibed none of the intrinsic qualities of his guru. Madhu Limaye on the other hand had the pretensions of being the intellectual heir of Lohia, the new ideologue of the Socialists. George, the fire-brand trade unionist, was like a tamed anarchist suddenly trying to show his worth as an efficient establishment man; quite a misplaced role for him. The whole culture and ethos of this tribe was of destruction. Champion party-breakers of Indian politics, they could only break, never build.

It was quite a menagerie that had come together as a direct result of Mrs Gandhi's Emergency rule. As was clear to all, except to these new rulers, it was the sheer anger and hatred against the Indira-Sanjay "dictatorship" which had brought them to power.

But the new euphoria that came with the fall of Mrs Gandhi blinded them to the reality of the situation, and within an hour of their solemn pledge at the Raj Ghat, the clash of egos had begun. Each one of the gerontocrats thought and behaved as though he himself had brought about the victory. Desai was acting the "Sarvochch" again. After all it was under his chairmanship that the Janata Party had won the victory and this was the time to pick up the thread where it had been lost years ago, when he had been denied his succession to the throne. He had always thought of himself as Nehru's logical heir, but he had been "cheated" by the machinations of "small men" in politics. He had repeatedly staked his claim to the prime ministership, but each time he had been thwarted by a "chit of a girl" who was "not suitable" for the office and whom he had considered his "duty" to oppose. Even more than him, Charan Singh considered himself the "architect" of not only the Janata Party but even more of its victory at the polls. The clean sweep from Amritsar to Patna, as he was to claim later, was entirely due to him. If anybody deserved the crown it was him. So also thought Jagjivan Ram, who had nursed as great an ambition to become the Prime Minister as Desai or Charan Singh. He had no doubt that the victory was entirely due to him. If he hadn't exploded his "bomb", Ram was convinced, Mrs Gandhi would have come back to power. Why had he left her if he couldn't become the PM even now? What was the point in all the fight against 'dictatorship' if he were to remain content with ministership? Even Mrs Gandhi would have given him that, and perhaps if he had bargained hard enough she might even have made him the Deputy Prime Minister. His sly aide, H.N. Bahuguna, felt even more frustrated, for he had hoped to rule the country from behind Babuji's chair. That indeed had been the expectation of his Russian friends who were said to have put so much money into the CFD election coffers.

But it was Charan Singh who was to prove the biggest threat to the unity of the Janata Party. Not even for a day was he reconciled to a second position in the party or the Government. His inflated ego was a problem even during the JP movement. When arrangements were going on for a demonstration before Parliament in March 1975, the Lok Sangharsha Samiti had printed posters giving the names of the Opposition leaders who were going to participate. Some of the posters were sent to the

BLD office, and when Charan Singh saw it he lost his temper. His name was second in the list of participants. "This is a conspiracy not to let me become Prime Minister," he fumed, although at that time to think of becoming Prime Minister was worse than a pipe-dream for any Opposition leader. The BLD office refused to accept the posters and eventually the Lok Sangharsha Samiti thought it wiser to get new ones printed with Charan Singh at the top of the list!

The strains and tensions began at the very beginning. Just two days after Mrs Gandhi announced her decision to go to the polls, the leaders of the then Opposition parties met in Delhi to discuss ways of giving the lady a joint fight. None except the BLD chief, Charan Singh was anxious for a merger of the parties. To Morarji Desai the very idea of merger was a "sin", and even those in the Congress (O) who were willing to talk about it would do so on their own terms. Though the Congress (O) had been reduced to a virtual cipher, its leaders talked haughtily about the long history and tradition of the Congress. If there was to be a merger let the others merge with the Congress (O), they insisted. To Charan Singh this was anathema. He just did not believe in joining any party of which he was not the chief. The Jan Sangh was careful not to show its hand, but it appeared the party leaders were agreeable to any step that would create a joint front against Mrs Gandhi. The debacle of the 1974 UP Assembly elections had convinced the Jan Sangh ideologues that the party by itself could not go beyond the point it had reached. Willy-nilly the party had come to be branded as a "communal and reactionary" organisation—a party of shopkeepers. The leaders had to give themselves a secular, progressive image if they were to make any headway in the country's politics. The party had to live down its stigma, it had to enlarge its base.

Charan Singh was a happy man when the idea of the Janata Party was finally accepted. He seemed to have taken it for granted that he would be the natural leader of the combine. Who else had striven so hard for it? He could hardly bear the shock when his own BLD comrade, Piloo Mody, proposed the name of Morarji Desai for chairmanship of the party. "You didn't propose my name because you are also a Gujarati," the furious Chaudhuri accused Mody later. It was as though his whole life had been wasted. That is what he told his supporters at the UP Nivas.

His men prodded him to go it alone, but which Opposition leader in January 1977 had the morale or the guts to fight Mrs Gandhi alone? Indeed, many of them had all the time been striving for a rapprochement with her. Charan Singh himself had written a conciliatory letter to Mrs Gandhi just five days before she announced the elections, and his aides had been holding secret parleys with Biju Patnaik who had established a pipeline with the Sanjay caucus. But Charan Singh was now claiming to be the founder of the Janata Party. He was furious at having been let down.

But the smooth, double-talking leaders of the Jan Sangh managed to mollify Charan Singh with sweet promises. They told him Morarji Desai was only being made the "Barooah of the Janata Party" and it was he who would become the party's Indira Gandhi. After consultations with his supporters he agreed to be the General Secretary of the party and word was sent to Atal Behari Vajpayee and L.K. Advani. The two Jan Sangh leaders went to Charan Singh, only to find the BLD leader in an aggressive mood: "Do you think I am so small as to become the Munshi of the party?" That was perhaps his strategy to ensure that he would at least get the second place in the party. Since he had described the post of General Secretary as that of a 'Munshi,' how about becoming the Vice-Chairman? All right, said Charan Singh, I would accept that, but on one condition : I mùst be given the unquestioned authority to conduct the elections in the whole of northern India.

The proposal was put forth by Jan Sangh leader, Bhairon Singh Shekhawat at one of the meetings of the new party. It was unpalatable to Desai. "The Chairman is naturally the overall incharge," he said. Chaudhuri said haltingly, "Let Morarji bhai look after the South, I shall look after North." Retorted Desai : "Why should I look after only the South? I am the all-India President." It appeared the whole thing would break right there, but with great difficulty Morarji agreed to make Charan Singh "incharge of northern States."

After the victory in the elections, Charan Singh thought he would be the unquestioned choice for prime ministership. Hadn't the Jan Sangh leaders promised him that? But as Charan Singh continued to bemoan for years, not one of them even suggested his name when he himself lay helpless in Willingdon Hospital.

Not even did his Sancho Panza, Raj Narain, suggest his name. Instead, he played on his deep-rooted antipathy towards Jagjivan Ram and H.N. Bahuguna and persuaded him to throw in his weight on the side of Morarji Desai. "That was the first great mistake I committed," Charan Singh said after he was dismissed from the ministry in June 1978. His "second great mistake," he said, was to "allow" Chandra Shekhar to become the president of the Janata Party. Having lost the crown, he had wanted to control at least the party. Karpoori Thakur was his choice for party presidentship. But came the 'directive' from JP, asking that Chandra Shekhar be named the first president of the party. If Jagjivan Ram could never forgive Jayaprakash Narayan for having "cheated" him of the prime ministership, nor could Charan Singh ever forgive JP for having "foisted" Chandra Shekhar as president of the party. "Who is this Chandra Shekhar? How dare he preside over a party which you created?" his supporters asked him. But as it happened, Charan Singh was hustled into accepting Chandra Shekhar, partly because he was told that Chandra Shekhar would only be a figurehead, and he the real boss. Having commanded the Janata Party to unprecedented success in the Lok Sabha elections, Charan Singh was confident that nobody could challenge his supremacy in the northern States, beyond which his vision, in any case, did not extend. The Jan Sangh, which had come back as the biggest single group in the Lok Sabha, was all too anxious to play ball with him, because the party could see that a BLD-Jan Sangh axis in the northern States would prove invincible—a profitable alliance. The Jan Sangh was soon to adopt a "two-tier" policy for itself: an alliance with Morarji Desai at the Centre and with Charan Singh in the northern States.

Charan Singh's first big clash with the party leadership came on the eve of the Assembly elections of 1977. He had expected the same supremacy again and had begun distributing tickets as he chose, only to find that he was no longer the supreme boss. His blood boiled when the party president, Chandra Shekhar, chopped 88 names from his list for Uttar Pradesh, a State which he had come to believe was as much his fief as Meerut once was. How dare anyone question his authority in Uttar Pradesh? A great one at writing resignation letters, Charan Singh promptly sent off his resignation as "observer" of Uttar Pradesh and withdrew from the Election Commission his letter authorizing the BLD symbol to the Janata Party. He thought this would be enough to cow them down, but contrary to his expectations, Chandra Shekhar took a tough line and issued an ultimatum. Charan Singh's "gun-point politics" having failed, Raj Narain flew like Prospero's Ariel to the Janata Party headquarters, retrieved the resignation letter and tore it up.

But this was only the beginning of the tug-of-war between the two camps. Within weeks of his becoming Home Minister, a regular durbar had started at Charan Singh's house. Among the principal courtiers were Raj Narain, Shyam Nandan Mishra, Dinesh Singh and Bhanu Pratap Singh. At most of these durbars the topic of discussion was Morarji Desai and his family. An anti-Desai atmosphere was being built up. S.N. Mishra, an old supporter of Desai, who had "defected" to Charan Singh out of his anger at not having been made a minister, launched a tirade against Kanti Desai in Parliament, quoting chapter and verse on his links with the Hinduja brothers and various other shady business connections. And still unknown to the people, Charan Singh had sent off a letter to Morarji Desai in March 1978, drawing the latter's attention to the reported stand he took at a public meeting at Bhavnagar on 15 January 1978, that the charges against Kanti Desai were "unfounded and mischievous." Maintaining that "most of the allegations against Mr Kanti Desai reverberating throughout the country are new and not old," Charan Singh had quoted Earl of Chatham, a former British Prime Minister, as having said that if allegations were made against a minister they should invariably be inquired into. He wanted that Desai should order an inquiry, for such a step alone would help maintain the "moral" of the party and the "good" name of the Government which were "going down steeply with every passing day."

Desai had shot back a reply saying that "interested persons were making propaganda against my son not so much to involve him but to ensure that I get out." He recalled that there were so many persons "insinuating" about Charan Singh's son-in-law but he had defended him in Parliament because he refused to believe them. And if it came to charges against his son, Desai too had a number of letters making allegations against Charan Singh, his son-in-law and his wife and if they were to follow the principle mentioned by Charan Singh "we should be appointing a number of commissions of inquiry every day. . . ."

In their fight with Desai, Charan Singh and Raj Narain were perhaps taking the Jan Sangh support for granted. The BLD-Jan Sangh alliance had achieved results and the two groups had grabbed the lion's share of power in the northern States. Charan Singh was willing to make further "concessions" to the Jan Sangh if only the latter would help him achieve his life's ambition. One day Charan Singh had called a Jan Sangh leader and proposed that they should "discuss further plans for the future." What plans? the Jan Sangh leader had asked, and Charan Singh had given him an "analysis" of the Indian political scene as he saw it. The sum and substance of it was that Morarji Desai could not give the right direction to the country. Nor could Chandra Shekhar handle the Janata Party. Both had completely failed in their jobs. The only solution, said Charan Singh, was that the Jan Sangh group should take the presidentship of the party and he himself should become the Prime Minister. "If I have the full support of your group," he said, "it can be done without any difficulty. Morarji must not be allowed to go on for long. You see, he has men like Bahuguna with him in the ministry. . . .I have told him so many times to remove him but he just does not listen."

Charan Singh had already sent off his "personal and confidential" letter to Desai accusing H.N. Bahuguna of being in close touch with the CPI and of trying to establish contacts with the USSR. "In fact he (Bahuguna) is regarded in some circles as an agent of the KGB. In 1974 and 1975 the USSR is reported to have thought of grooming him as a possible successor to Smt. Indira Gandhi. It was upon this realization on the part of the Congress leadership that he was unceremoniously removed from the chief ministership of Uttar Pradesh at the end of 1975 although he enjoyed a majority both in the Congress Party and the legislature."

Charan Singh's proposal had not come as a surprise to the Jan Sangh leader; he was well aware of the Home Minister's "one-point programme": to become the Prime Minister. But he had remained non-committal, saying the whole thing would have to be discussed at length with other leaders of the group. Charan Singh, however, took it as a sort of consent and gave the green signal to his "Hanuman." The battle was begun the very day Morarji Desai left on his American tour on 5 June 1978. After a long discussion with the Home Minister, who was convalescing at the All India Institute of Medical Sciences, Raj Narain returned to his office, called a press conference and launched his attack on Chandra Shekhar, the National Executive and the Janata Parliamentary Board. These were all ad hoc committees, he said, and must be scrapped. Day after day he continued his onslaught, adding new charges against Chandra Shekhar every time he met the press. He described him as an 'illegal president' and accused him of hobnobbing with people who were talking about a third force against the Janata Party. Just about that time Chandra Shekhar had gone to a camp held at Narora to discuss the state of affairs in the Janata Party and a possible alternative to it. The camp was only one of the manifestations of the all-round disenchantment with the new Government which had shown no indication of getting down to the urgent problems facing the country.

The Industries Minister, George Fernandes, had himself submitted a Note to the party's National Executive, admitting that there was a gradual erosion of the party and the Government, and "all of us are guilty of thinking and acting as members of the merging parties rather than as members of one political party." Referring indirectly to the warring triumvirate at the top, Fernandes had called upon Morarji Desai, Charan Singh and Jagjivan Ram to "exercise jointly their political and moral authority to keep the party in shape. . . .This they owe to the country, to the party and to posterity. If they fail the consequences will be tragic for everone. . . ."

That was a tall order for leaders who were chipping relentlessly at their own credibility, without any concern for the mounting disorder all around them. Harijans and Muslims were under attack in different parts of the country; higher education had virtually collapsed—47 universities had been closed for various lengths of time between April 1977 and January 1978; and in the factories during the same period, 1,363 strikes and 199 lockouts had resulted in a loss of production worth Rs 83 crores. But the great leaders of the Janata Party were busy pulling one another down. Desai never tired of privately condemning Jagjivan Ram for "private immorality and corruption,"[1] Ram was openly describing

[1]Madhu Limaye wrote in *Mainstream*, Annual Number 1979: "Desai's hypocrisy knows no limit. While publicly supporting Ram's claim for forming a government, privately he has been denouncing Ram in strong words saying,'I

Charan Singh as a "Kulak leader," making a butt of him in an interview, of all persons to Maneka Gandhi:[2]

JR : Why do you find Charan Singh so important? (Laughter)
MG: Well, Charan Singh is important because he is the Home Minister!
JR : So was Brahmanand Reddi. (Laughter)

While the patchwork-party was rapidly falling apart, a no-holds-barred infighting was on. Listen to one of the party's most important General Secretaries, Ramakrishna Hegde:

The purpose... of Charan Singh and the constituent led by him was to reach the top as has been candidly admitted by him. His life's ambition was to become Prime Minister. It was neither the transformation of society nor the elimination of exploitation, nor even the well-being of the people. The objective was purely personal. If the Janata Party had failed to get majority in 1977, Charan Singh would surely have joined Indira Gandhi within weeks after the elections. Therefore, from the very beginning we found that an open and shameless struggle for power was started by one constituent unit and through sickening character assas-sination. Whether it was in the ranking and distribution of portfolios or it was distribution of tickets to party candidates, unprincipled equations based on naked personal ambitions domi-nated the scene. For those engaged in this competition of self-promotion, the election pledges, the party's declared policies and programmes became irrelevant. Even JP was forgotten. There was hardly any serious discussion in the National Execu-tive on the implementation of the poll pledges, economic policies and the problems of the people. An atmosphere of cold war made it impossible to have any constructive and productive deliberation. The Central Parliamentary Board functioned like the Security Council and a particular member constantly exer-cised the veto power....

And so, when Raj Narain began his concerted attacks against

---

shall never allow that man who lacks private morality and public integrity to become the Prime Minister."
[2]In *Surya*, May 1978.

the Party president nobody had any doubt about the objective. It was clearly meant to force him to resign from the presidentship so that the next part of the "master plan" could be put through. But in between came the statement of one of the prominent Jan Sangh leaders, Sunder Singh Bhandari, clearly indicating for the first time the attitude of the group. Bhandari accepted that the BLD and the Jan Sangh had come to an "arrangement" when Chief Ministers were chosen in 1977. He, however, added that there was no inbuilt continuity and "none of us can take each other for granted in our respective designs." Bhandari also rejected Raj Narain's accusation that the National Executive was illegal and described the differences in the party as "personal, involving no policy or principle." What was more, Bhandari made it clear that the Jan Sangh group would [not support any no-confidence motion against Morarji Desai. Next day reporters | drew Raj Narain's attention to the statement, but he said, "Don't try to start a quarrel between us and the Jan Sangh. You won't succeed in the game." Raj Narain, the RSS-baiter, was still to be born.

Desai was furious when he returned from abroad. He scoffed at the "attar" Raj Narain wanted to apply on him, and instead reprimanded him for the foul smell he had been spreading during his trip abroad. Desai had not failed to see that it was he who was the real target of Raj Narain's attacks. On 22 June, the National Executive charged Raj Narain with violating the party's directive not to air intra-party differences in public. At this Charan Singh realized that the Raj Narain affair was not quite the issue on which he should take a stand, and so he swiftly found a new pretext for damning the Desai Government. In the midnight of 28 June he fired his salvo from Suraj Kund, a holiday resort to which he had moved for recuperating his health, describing the Government (of which he himself was still a part) as a "pack of impotent people" who could not govern the country. "Perhaps those who differ from me," he said in his statement, "do not realize sufficiently the intensity of feelings among the people of our country on the Government's failure to put the former Prime Minister behind the bars by now. They draw all sorts of conclusions and are inclined to give credence to all kinds of stories. . . ." He said a section of the people wanted that Mrs Gandhi should be detained under MISA. . .If the Government did this, he said, hundreds of mothers of Emergency victims would celebrate the occasion like Diwali. . ."Of course in any other country she would have by now been facing a trial on the lines of the historic Nuremburg trial..." Charan Singh had perhaps forgotten his *faux pas* of October 1977 and that he himself was still the Home Minister, responsible for dealing with the cases against Mrs Gandhi. Besides, there was the propriety of a Minister issuing such a statement against his own Government. As Morarji Desai pointed out in the letter demanding his resignation, at no stage had the Home Minister consulted his Cabinet colleagues or him before issuing the statement. This, he said, amounted to a violation of the principle of collective responsibility and was against all norms and practices of the parliamentary system. Raj Narain was also asked to resign for his behaviour in Simla where he had violated Section 144 and attacked the Janata Chief Minister of Himachal Pradesh. A day after submitting his resignation, Charan Singh expressed his relief "because in the Government I was surrounded by many corrupt persons." His expression of "relief" was about as credible as Mrs Gandhi's "utter, utter relief" on knowing that she had been defeated in the March '77 elections!

"These people cannot govern the country," Mrs Gandhi was now telling her interviewers gleefully. But she was not the only one to be heartened by the growing rifts in the Janata Party. Also delighted were the CPI and the Russian lobby in the country. They felt encouraged by every discomfiture that the Government faced. The Russians had obviously been disturbed by the turn of events in the country. The last year or so of the Emergency had not at all been propitious for the pro-Russian Communists in the country. Things had come to a head between Mrs Gandhi and her CPI allies over Sanjay Gandhi's personality and policies. Her message was clear : if the CPI found it necessary or expedient to support her, it would have to do so at *her* terms and that the CPI had to shed its belief that it could meddle in the Congress Party affairs with impunity. Her attack was followed by a flurry of statements by other Congressmen denouncing the CPI. The Communists had gone about telling the people that the CIA had got around Sanjay Gandhi himself in order to "destroy" Mrs Gandhi. Various names of CIA agents and links were talked about. An American reporter even flew to India to study the activities of one of the U.S. officials in the Embassy who was said to have established contacts with

Sanjay Gandhi. The Indian names mentioned were of Kuldip Narang and Farooq Abdullah, the politically ambitious son of Sheikh Abdullah. Both were close friends and supporters of Sanjay Gandhi, and certainly had very friendly relations with the Americans. Mrs Gandhi herself was said to have had close links with the CIA at one time, as the revelations made by the former U.S. Ambassador to India, Daniel Patrick Moynihan were to suggest. "We had twice, but only twice, interfered in Indian politics to the extent of providing money to a political party. Both times it was done in the face of a prospective Communist victory in a state election, once in Kerala and once in West Bengal. . . .Both times the money was given to the Congress Party, which had asked for it. Once it was given to Mrs Gandhi herself, who was then a party official."[3]

When Moynihan's book was published in India, one year after it was out all over the world, it created a political furore, and Mrs Gandhi took to the usual recourse of politicians in such a situation: a bland denial. "It is a baseless and mischievous statement," she told newsmen at the Chandigarh airport on way to Jammu.[4] "They (the Americans) are against me and it is well known."

The denial by Mrs Gandhi and the others involved, including S.K. Patil who had been the party Treasurer at that time, provoked Moynihan to give out further details. He reiterated the payments and said the funds involved were "of the size one would expect from a serious campaign contributor," which thought the correspondent reporting him,[5] would suggest figures of between $10,000 and $100,000. "At the time the payments were made it was reasonable for the American Government to equate the Government of India with the Congress Party," Moynihan said. "We made billions of dollars in contribution to the Government of India; so it didn't seem all that different, I imagine, to contribute to the political party that dominated the Government 20 years ago. . . .They asked for help twice and the American Government gave it." Moynihan had gone on to say that the two paragraphs in his book that dealt with the political contributions had to be cleared with the CIA before publication—"just a couple of lines took me an entire working day to get clearance."

[3] Daniel Patrick Moynihan in *A Dangerous Place.*
[4] *The Times of India*, 12 April 1978.
[5] Simon Winchester in *The Guardian*, 28 April 1979.

But times had changed when Moynihan himself came as the Ambassador to India in 1973. "I had no great success. Under the rule of Nehru's daughter, the world's largest democracy had, in foreign affairs, become bound to Soviet policy. Worse, it was drifting into an authoritarianism all its own. With my own Government collapsing at home, the most I could do was to set about liquidating the extraordinary demi-Raj that the United States had established in India in the nineteen-fifties and sixties. Rather as the British had, I hoped to march out rather than be driven out."[6]

Right after the Congress split in 1969, when Mrs Gandhi led a minority Government and needed the votes of Communist MPs to survive, the Communists had started manipulating the Congress affairs to their own advantage. Years ago, in the mid-sixties, Mohan Kumaramangalam, a shrewd tactician and lawyer, had submitted to the CPI leadership his "thesis" entitled *A Review of the Party Policy since 1947*, stressing the futility of the party policy of a leftist United Front to "break the monopoly of power of the Congress Party." He had instead suggested a plan to capture the Congress itself from within. His thesis, however, remained a dead letter for years, until the time seemed ripe for it. After the general elections of 1967, the Congress strength in the Lok Sabha was reduced from 361 to 283 and its position was further worsened after the split of 1969. Kumaramangalam again brought out his thesis and found greater acceptance for it this time. In the next few years nearly a dozen known Communists and fellow-travellers intruded into the Congress and began playing a crucial role in the affairs of the party, so much so that at one time Kumaramangalam was almost on the verge of becoming the Deputy Prime Minister and there was even a talk about a possible Congress-CPI coalition at the Centre.

But it so happened that Mohan Kumaramangalam's life was suddenly cut short in a plane accident in the summer of 1973. All the hopes that the Russians and their friends in India had put in the man were dashed to the ground. The other Congress leader who was gradually coming close to the Russians in those years was L.N. Mishra, but he too died at the height of his political power and influence. Then it was the turn of H.N. Bahuguna and Mrs

[6]Moynihan in *A Dangerous Place*.

Nandini Satpathy to be picked up for "grooming" by the Russians. Unlike Satpathy, Bahuguna did not have a Communist background, unless being a trade union leader of rickshawallahs and electricity workers could have made up for it. But he did fairly well during the time that he was Chief Minister in Uttar Pradesh. Aware of the importance of having a direct line with the Soviet Union, Bahuguna had assiduously wooed the Russian Ambassador in Delhi. He invited him to Lucknow and threw a big party in his honour. Bahuguna had also participated enthusiastically in a big jamboree of the Indo-Soviet Cultural Society. So impressed was the Russian envoy with Bahuguna's dynamism and his "progressive ideas" that he hailed him as a "great leader of the Indian people" and several Russian officers were heard saying that Bahuguna was the "future Prime Minister of India." But that, according to Charan Singh at least, put an end to his chief ministership. The same happened to Nandini Satpathy, who as the Chief Minister of Orissa, had gone high in the list of Congressmen "close to Russia." Was it just a coincidence, many wondered, that Mrs Gandhi's axe fell on anybody who happened to get too close to the Soviet Union?

Though the CPI and the Russian lobby in the Congress had been highly suspicious and critical of Sanjay Gandhi, they had enthusiastically welcomed the clamping of the Emergency and the incarceration of Jayaprakash Narayan and hundreds of Opposition leaders behind him. The CPI had been the first to raise a cry against "Fascist JP" and had for long been egging Mrs Gandhi to take stern action against the movement in Bihar. But as the Emergency developed and the "CIA-backed caucus" took hold of the eyes and ears of Mrs Gandhi, the Communists fell into a great dilemma—though they were all for the lady, the son was an "untouchable" and when they tried to draw a line between the two the lady came down with a "keep off" warning. With the Soviet leadership still enamoured of the lady, there was little their creatures in India could do except fret and fume. One way they could show their anger was to keep out the name of Sanjay from all their publications, as though they were putting up a fight against the young upstart.

The political "earthquake" of March 1977 left the Russian leadership gasping. They were hard put to decide what to do. Even on the day of polling (16 March), the *Pravda* had run an article praising Mrs Gandhi's "impressive successes scored, particularly in recent.times. . ." and Moscow's radio station, *Peace and Progress—Voice of the Soviet People*, said that no amount of "demogogy" on the part of the Rightists would be able to weaken the resolve of the workers, peasants, small businessmen and intellectuals to vote for the Congress. But on the morning after Mrs Gandhi relinquished office, the Voice of the Soviet People attributed her defeat to the "mistakes and excesses of the Emergency."

Clearly, the Soviet Government had been caught off-guard by the defeat of Mrs Gandhi, and were trying hard to retrace their steps. Though everybody seemed to say that the new Government headed by Morarji Desai was clearly pro-America and certainly the new Foreign Minister, Atal Behari Vajpayee could be nothing but anti-Russia, the Soviet Government had to try for at least a working, if not warm, relationship with the Indian Government. After all, India had proved to be Russia's most loyal, stable and powerful client in the Third World, and it would not be politic to let it pass into the American sphere of influence. Within two days of the election results, the Soviet official organ, *Izvestia*, published an article criticising Mrs Gandhi's authoritarian behaviour during the Emergency. The country's Foreign Affairs Weekly, *Za Rubezhom*, was even more critical, not only of Mrs Gandhi but also of Sanjay Gandhi, both of whom had been welcomed on Soviet land like royal visitors only some months earlier.

The visits of Morarji Desai and Atal Behari Vajpayee to the Soviet Union in October 1977 allayed the Russian fears to some extent, but they could not be confident that the gains made in India would not be offset by the Janata Government's tilt towards America. New friends had to be made in the new ruling party. There were already some who had gone over to the Janata, such as H. N. Bahuguna and Nandini Satpathy, but while contacts with them had to be reinforced, new "vehicles" had to be spotted.

The first possible ally they could think of was Madhu Limaye, a man reputed to be one of the "ideologues" of the Janata Party. Though he had not joined the Government, he was no doubt going to be important in determining the policies and programmes of the party, not only by virtue of his being one of the general secretaries of the party (a highly rated position in the Soviet Union) but also because he had established himself as an effective parliamentarian.

Limaye had started courting the Russians several years ago. In 1973, when Leonid Brezhnev visited India, he had called on him in New Delhi to discuss "democracy" with the Soviet leader. Soon after the new Government came to power, Limaye led a delegation of the Indo-Soviet Cultural Society to Moscow, and he made quite a mark on the Russians. Back from Russia, Madhu had plunged himself wholeheartedly into a battle against the RSS scourge, knowing full well what it would do to the Janata Party. Only two years earlier when the question of non-Congress parties coming together was being discussed the then Socialist Party of Maharashtra had held a special session at Pune. There, Limaye had been the most ardent advocate of unity with the Jan Sangh and had even quoted Lohia that the "patriotism and nationalism of Jan Sangh, the egalitarian ethos of the Socialist Party and the legacy of the leadership of the freedom struggle of Congress (O) would together produce a beautiful blend." Since Limaye could not possibly attack the Jan Sangh directly, as it was an integral part of the Janata Party, he had decided to strike at the mother organisation of the group, something that he knew the Jan Sangh members would not take. Shrewd that he was, Madhu Limaye could see that the non-Jan Sanghis would not be able to capture the Janata Party organisation in the event of elections; the better organised RSS cadre would simply swamp them. And so within months of the Janata Party's formal launching he started saying that there could be no organisational elections in the party in the next five years and after that of course there would be no question of elections because the party itself would not be there.

Around the same time that Madhu Limaye went on his first trip to Moscow after the elections, another Janata Party MP, Devendra Satpathy, was invited to visit the German Democratic Republic. But instead of him, his wife, Nandini Satpathy went on the invitation, and it was while she was on her "goodwill mission" that her houses in Orissa and New Delhi were searched and a lot of "incriminating" materials seized. Mrs Satpathy was arrested and bailed out on return from GDR, and she at once called a press conference to declare that she was a "victim of the politics of terror, humiliation and character assassination." Twenty-six Janata Party MPs from various States, however, demanded that Mrs Satpathy should be dropped from the National Executive to "save the good name of the party." They said there had been reports in almost all the newspapers that the searches in her houses and those of people close to her had led to the discovery of cash beyond her known sources of income, jewellery, big bank accounts, unlicensed arms, foreign currencies and various incriminating documents including a secret script of a secret agency titled TISA. One English weekly even reported that currency notes worth Rs 51,000 bearing serial number in numerical order as well as the "Calcutta office stamp of a Consulate of a Communist country" had been recovered from Mrs Satpathy's Dhenkanal house in Orissa. It was hardly credible that the Consulate concerned would have been so foolish as to stamp the packets of currency notes before passing them on to Mrs Satpathy or that any sensible person would accept such tell-tale material. Certainly it was inconceivable that a shrewd politician like Mrs Satpathy who had such powerful enemies like Biju Patnaik would have committed any such blunder, but surprisingly enough, the report in the weekly had not been questioned or contradicted. But even if the story of stamped notes was all cooked up, there were other incriminating materials which the MPs thought were enough to throw her out of the National Executive. They, however, forgot that Mrs Satpathy had very powerful friends and protectors, including Babu Jagjivan Ram and the party president, Chandra Shekhar, himself. In spite of all the opposition from the Janata Godfather, Jayaprakash Narayan, who had gone on record to say that he knew "nothing good about Nandini Satpathy," she had been given the party ticket in the Orissa Assembly elections and continued to remain a member of the National Executive.

Within hours of her press conference, Satpathy had driven to 12 Willingdon Crescent. Unfortunately for her there was a press photographer waiting there, and much as Mrs Satpathy tried to hide her face, the camera clicked. "No, don't do that," Mrs Satpathy had shouted. She obviously did not want the whole world to know that she had gone to meet Mrs Gandhi. When she came out, this time with Mrs Gandhi and Mrs Mohsina Kidwai, the photographer again sought to take their pictures, but Nandini yelled, "I warned you, don't." Mrs Gandhi smiled as Nandini rushed into her car, hiding her face. Nothing suited the former Prime Minister better than if everybody knew that a member of the Janata National Executive had gone to her stealthily. When the news came out next day, everybody thought Nandini had gone to meet Mrs Gandhi because of the raids and the arrest, but there was obviously more to it than that. The plans to destabilize the Janata Government from within had already started.

Nandini had also gone to her friends, Jagjivan Ram and H.N. Bahuguna, to convince them to take a stand against the Janata Party which was "nothing but a Jan Sangh-RSS party." Both Ram and Bahuguna were already disenchanted with their position in the Government and even regretted having merged the CFD with the Janata Party, but they did not have the guts to leave their jobs, for that is what it would have come to if they took a position against Morarji Desai. They knew they would be given the order of the boot the day they showed any defiance.

Bahuguna had tried it one day but had been so badly snubbed that from then on he thought it wiser to stay mum. It was an informal meeting of the Cabinet on the eve of Vajpayee's visit to China. Chandra Shekhar and Nanaji Deshmukh had also been invited to attend. Soon after the meeting began, Bahuguna started opposing the China visit vehemently, maintaining that it would only create problems for India's relations with Russia, a country which had proved itself as our best friends. As he went on with his praise of Russia, Morarji Desai remarked: "Why are you always flattering the USSR?" Enraged, Bahuguna retorted: "You too are called pro-American by many." A tense silence pervaded the room for a while, and Nanaji Deshmukh tried to lighten the atmosphere by saying that everybody present was patriotic and nationalist. But Bahuguna cut him short and said sharply: "Don't be non-serious." Then Chandra Shekhar, who had been quiet all the while, lashed out at Bahuguna and kept it up for ten full minutes. That silenced Bahuguna.

Madhu Limaye, however, was not to be silenced by allegations that he was playing the Russian game. He did not care. He went ahead with the task he had taken upon himself: to oust Morarji Desai, and for this there was no better way than to hit out at Desai's Jan Sangh supporters. After his return from Russia, Madhu started cultivating Charan Singh in a big way. At that time Charan Singh was still in alliance with the Jan Sangh, but Madhu was all the time trying to wean him away from them, prodding him to join the war against the "Fascist RSS." But neither Charan Singh nor Raj Narain was ready for that yet.

Madhu in the meantime was also trying hard to cultivate Atal

Behari Vajpayee, hoping that he would be able to win him over to his point of view. A business house of Delhi, known to be friends of the Russian camp, had been put on the job of winning over Atal Behari Vajpayee and efforts were also made to cultivate Mrs Kaul, a family friend who lived with the Foreign Minister. At one point, one of the newspapers got Subramaniam Swamy to write an article attacking Vajpayee and his foreign policy, and it so happened that one of the correspondents who was close to Madhu Limaye showed the script to him several days before its publication. Limaye straight went to Vajpayee and told him the contents of the Swamy article. This was all part of Limaye's effort to ingratiate himself with Vajpayee, which he gave up only after the China visit was announced.

The biggest impetus to Limaye's operations came when Charan Singh crawled back into the Desai Government, leaving Raj Narain in the lurch. "See what I'll do now," proclaimed an incensed Raj Narain. His avowed aim from then on was either to pull down the Morarji Government or persuade Charan Singh to quit the Janata Party and revive the BLD. As far as the first aim was concerned, it coincided with the objective of Madhu Limaye. From then on it became a joint operation, with Raj Narain playing the cat's paw. Limaye convinced Raj Narain that the first thing to do was to join the battle against the RSS, and now there was no question of any hesitation on his part. He had been let down by the Jan Sangh, and he would show them the havoc he could create.

Raj Narain knew as well as Limaye that it was futile trying to capture the Janata Party organisation. He had taken away over four lakh membership forms from the party office, but it was one thing to take the forms and quite another to enrol members. Because of their disciplined RSS cadres the Jan Sangh group had done fast work in the enrolment of members and it was obvious that they would be in a dominating position in the event of an organisational election. Raj Narain and Limaye started a campaign for the postponement of party elections, alleging that 50 per cent or more of the new members were "bogus." On 11 March 1979, Raj Narain announced at Patna that the members of the BLD would form parallel units of the party at different levels. He said his group had taken the decision because of the "bogus" members enrolled by the Jan Sangh group.

By now Raj Narain had even started talking international affairs, now welcoming the Indo-USSR joint statement and now attacking Atal Behari Vajpayee for having accepted the sovereignty of China over Tibet. He was obviously parroting his comrade-in-arms, Madhu Limaye, who had found in Raj Narain a most useful front man, capable of a bluntness which was beyond him. Aiding and abetting Raj Narain's tirade against Morarji Desai and the RSS was his "press attache" Rajinder Puri whose excellent talents as a cartoonist had been ruined by his political and other non-journalistic ambitions. Soon after the Janata Party was formed, Puri had approached some of the Janata leaders and offered to do the publicity work for them during the elections. They thought he would be an asset to their poll propaganda and so agreed to take him on as their publicity man. But then he started pressing for full-fledged secretaryship of the party. Surendra Mohan and some other Janata leaders objected, but Morarji had been impressed by Puri's talents ever since he had drawn a complimentary cartoon of him in *The Statesman* during a leadership contest against Mrs Gandhi in which he had shown her as a puny lady standing high atop tier upon tier of other Congress leaders, with Morarji standing alongside all by himself, the loser no doubt but very much on his own strength. When the issue of Puri came up, Morarji said all right, let him have it, and so Puri was made the General Secretary No. 5 in-charge of publicity. But it turned out that he could do very little and the party had to arrange a separate publicity wing directly handled by Surendra Mohan. Even so, the unexpected victory of the Janata Party gave further spurt to the ambitions of the cartoonist-turned-pamphleteer and he began trying hard to become the Press Secretary to Prime Minister Desai. When he failed to get that, he was utterly disappointed. Even his general secretaryship was gone. In sheer frustration, he went to Nanaji Deshmukh and gave him a big talk on how the public relations of the Deendayal Upadhyaya Research Institute should be organised and how the Jan Sangh group itself needed the right kind of "image projection." Wasn't it sad that the group's successes at the polls were never quite proportionate to its real strength among the people? After all these preliminaries, he came up with the generous offer to undertake the publicity work for the whole group, and tried to impress upon Nanaji Deshmukh what a great work he could do for them with the "powerful

columns" he had in several top magazines of the country. All he
wanted in return was reimbursement of his monthly expenses—just
about five thousand rupees a month. When the 'offer' was turned
down by Deshmukh, Puri approached Raj Narain. He had at
last hit upon the right man. With all his publicised allergy towards
English, Raj Narain had a real weakness for somebody who could
draft his statements in presentable English, and Puri with his background of a cartoonist could use *Rajnarainics* in his language too.
The 'pack of impotents' statement was perhaps the first master-
piece of Puri after he was hired by the Raj Narain-Charan Singh
camp. And so, armed with an excellent publicist like Puri, Raj
Narain was all set for his anti-Morarji battle.

Madhu Limaye in the meantime had been working hard to build
a bridge between Charan Singh and H.N. Bahuguna, who had for
long been political foes in Uttar Pradesh politics. Limaye tried to
convince Charan Singh that with Bahuguna on their side they
would be able to make successful inroads into the Muslim votes.
As Chief Minister of UP, this clever politician from the Garhwal
hills had been a great hit with the Muslims of the State, from the
Nawabs and the Begums to the poorest of them. Bahuguna had a
knack of speaking in Urdu, interspersed with *shar-o-shaeri* which
went very well with the Muslim audiences. The great PR man that
he was, he would go to the Muslim homes, sit down to eat with
them and soon be on the closest of terms. Limaye was quite aware
of the great potential of the man, and of course he knew that if
his Russian friends would back anyone for the future leadership of
the country it would be Bahuguna. But the mutual suspicions
and antipathies between Charan Singh and Bahuguna were so deep-
rooted that it took Limaye quite a lot of convincing on both sides.
Neither had forgotten the letters they had written to Morarji
Desai about each other. And yet, Madhu's arguments made sense
to both. Bahuguna, who had for long been stewing in his own juice,
could see that he had been driven back to the wall in his own home
State, from which he some day aspired to become Prime Minister.
He realised that the position of the respective parties in Uttar
Pradesh, in case of elections, could be first Indira Congress,
second Charan Singh's BLD, third Jan Sangh and fourth his own.
A dismal prospect. Being part of a rag-bag coalition of which the
Jan Sangh was the major partner, even his popularity among the
Muslims was fast eroding. He just could not take positions which

would keep his Muslim following intact. He had not even been able to go to Aligarh during its worst days of rioting. Pragmatic that he was, he could see that if he wanted to become even the second political force in Uttar Pradesh, he would have to join hands with Charan Singh. Perhaps if the two came together they could even blunt the threat of Mrs Gandhi. But would the Jat leader really accept him as his second man? It was here that Madhu Limaye played his cards. When he first put the suggestion across to Charan Singh, some time in April 1978, the latter rejected it outright. It was only after he had gone into his six-month political oblivion as a result of the Jan Sangh's "stab in the back" that Charan Singh was more responsive to Limaye's suggestion.

The deal was finally struck when Charan Singh told Bahuguna, "I have a son, but you know he is not interested in politics. After me my following will be yours." That became the basis for an understanding between the two former foes. Thereafter, Bahuguna tried to bring about a rapprochement between Morarji Desai and Charan Singh, but it was scuttled at that stage. For its own reasons, the Jan Sangh was anxious to play the leading role in bringing the two together. Though they had ditched Charan Singh and plumped for Morarji as a better bet to keep the Government going the Jan Sangh leaders were also worried about the possibility of Charan Singh quitting the party and thereby destabilizing the Government. Eventually, the Chandra Sekhar-Nanaji-Hegde combine succeeded in selling the idea of deputy prime ministership to Charan Singh. Morarji agreed, but decided he would promote Jagjivan Ram to deputy prime ministership along with Charan Singh. That was a game very similar to the one Jawaharlal Nehru had played on Desai in the early sixties. After the death of Govind Ballabh Pant in 1961, the question of electing a deputy leader of the Congress Parliamentary Party had arisen, and Desai had learnt to his dismay that Jagjivan Ram had been put up as a candidate. After the passing away of Maulana Azad and Govind Ballabh Pant, Morarji had come to be No. 2 in the cabinet, and he reminded Nehru that it was the accepted convention that the No. 2 man became the deputy leader. Nehru then proposed electing two deputy leaders, one from the Lok Sabha, and the other from the Rajya Sabha. Desai told Jawaharlal: "If you had made this proposal to Sardar Patel, he would have resigned from the cabinet. I have so far observed the rule that I should accept a position in the party only if I am unanimously elected to it. If, therefore, there is a contest for deputy leadership, I will not stand for election, and I feel that I must resign from the cabinet." Nehru told him it was difficult for him to persuade Ram not to contest. Morarji was in a fix. He could see that they had decided to have a contest, because they knew that Morarji would prefer to leave the race if he was not unanimously elected. But he was not going to give in so easily. He told Nehru that in that case he would contest the election. "The general atmosphere," Desai wrote in *The Story of My Life*, "was that I would have been elected, and Jawaharlalji changed his tactics and asked me whether I had any objection if no Minister became deputy leader, and one ordinary member from the Lok Sabha and another from the Rajya Sabha were elected as deputy leaders." Eventually, Nehru had taken that decision, and Desai had no doubt in his mind that all these plans had only been meant to prevent him from becoming the deputy leader.

Morarji was now trying something similar on Charan Singh. Incensed by the move, which he could see was meant to belittle him, Charan Singh made one of his many memorable statements : "The issue of my joining the Government stands closed—and closed finally."

Within weeks, Charan Singh took oath as Deputy Prime Minister, along with Jagjivan Ram. Poor Raj Narain, who had done so much jumping and shouting for his leader was left high and dry. Right then he told some of his supporters that henceforth his sole objective would be to pull down the Desai Government. No price was going to be too big for achieving that objective, not even a surrender to Mrs Gandhi and Sanjay. The lady, who was by then in deep trouble, had already sent out feelers to all and sundry. From the Tihar Jail, she had sent a big bouquet to Charan Singh on his birthday. Both had been in trouble then. Charan Singh was fighting a last-ditch battle against Desai, and he thought the mighty display of his power at the kisan rally would shake the Government. His Jat supporters were itching for a confrontation with Morarji Desai, never mind if it meant aligning themselves with Mrs Gandhi. "Once Chaudhuri Saheb and Indira Gandhi come together no force can defeat them," was the refrain in the Jatlands of Uttar Pradesh and Haryana. The combination would have come about after the rally itself, had the "doves" in Charan Singh's camp not succeeded in persuading him to join as Deputy Prime Minister.

Raj Narain was now only too keen for an understanding with Mrs Gandhi. The pipelines were already there. For quite some time, at least half a dozen persons had been trying hard to renew a dialogue between the Charan Singh camp and the Gandhi family. There was Swarup Singh, a former Vice-Chancellor of Delhi University, who was a relative of Charan Singh and a close personal friend of Bansi Lal. With the help of Devi Lal he had now become a member of the Rajya Sabha. Then there was Brahma Dutt, a former lieutenant of Charan Singh, who was now a member of Mrs Gandhi's party. There were Kuldip Narang and his cartoonist friend, Rajinder Puri, nursing a grudge against Morarji Desai. And then there was B.P. Maurya, who had as close links with some of the supporters of Charan Singh as he had with Mrs Gandhi. All of them had been trying in their own ways to build a bridge between the two leaders. In a way, Raj Narain had already collaborated with Sanjay Gandhi in the propagation of the Suresh-Sushama pictures. While Raj Narain's Kisan Sammelan had managed the wall poster showing the two in Kama Sutra style poses, Maneka Gandhi had put them lovingly on the cover of her magazine. A series of meetings between Raj Narain and Sanjay Gandhi followed, and there were times when the great "giant-killer of Rae Bareli" had to wait for hours in his car outside 12 Willingdon Crescent to meet the chief of the defunct Maruti. Raj Narain insisted there was "nothing political" about his meetings with Sanjay Gandhi, and yet everybody knew there was more to it than Sanjay congratulating Raj Narain on his anti-RSS jehad.

The first big salvo of the Raj Narain-Madhu Limaye jehad was fired when the Jan Sangh men were thrown out of the Uttar Pradesh Government. Jagjivan Ram, too, went along with the Raj Narain-Bahuguna plan to some extent. For one thing, Ram did not have much hold over the CFD in Uttar Pradesh. For another, Bahuguna argued with Ram that it would be good strategy to bring down Ram Naresh Yadav, so that Charan Singh would realise his dependence on them. Moreover, they decided that the next Chief Minister would not be a BLD man, which was why Banarsi Das got the job. What worried Morarji and his supporters most was the *volte face* of Bahuguna. It was largely as a reaction to this that they decided to topple Karpoori Thakur in

Bihar. To begin with, the party president was not in favour of the move for he did not want to create yet another enemy at that stage. Chandra Shekhar's argument was that it would be dangerous to have two backward leaders in opposition at the same time. But then the ambitions of the Rajput mafia in Bihar got the better of such arguments and Karpoori Thakur was ousted.

The last act in the "Operation Morarji" actually started after the fall of Karpoori Thakur and Devi Lal. Raj Narain had now two strong allies, both of whom had supported Charan Singh during his days of trouble. Charan Singh had done nothing for them when both were struggling for survival. Matters came to a head on 12 June when Raj Narain was removed from the National Executive of the Janata Party for one year as a punishment for his personal attacks on his party colleagues and his public criticism of Government policies. Raj Narain, who was having his meetings with Devaraj Urs in Bangalore that day, described it as a "political action" and went on in his own characteristic style to say that "I am for the people, by the people and of the people ... nobody can remove me from the people. The news is not hot for me." Charan Singh was holidaying at Simla. All he said was : "No comments."

Next day the Central Disciplinary Committee of the Janata Party issued show-cause notices to Chief Minister Devi Lal and the Haryana Janata Party chief, Mrs Chandravati, asking them to explain their conduct in the Narnaul Assembly elections, where they had openly sabotaged the election campaign of the party candidate.

Events were moving fast on the Opposition front, too. The parting of ways between Mrs Gandhi and Devaraj Urs was having its own political fall-out. For once the impression went round that the lady had been cornered, driven to the wall. Everybody thought her fortunes were going downhill. The only *raison d'etre* for the rag-bag Janata combine staying together was at last over, or so it seemed. For almost the whole of 28 months that the Janata Party had been in power, its leaders had gone round and round the great mulberry bush that was Indira Gandhi. All the time she had remained their major preoccupation, as though their very lives depended on her going up or down, and it was largely the fear of her return which had kept them from flying into different directions.

But now that the lady's threat had receded, or seemingly so, there was a burst of activity inside the various groups of the Janata Party. Madhu Limaye was now on to his game in a big way. He organised a meeting on 17 May to explore the possibility of the dream he had been striving to realize—the possibility of left unity in the country. Among those who attended were C. Rajeswara Rao, Bhupesh Gupta, P. Ramamurthy and Basavapunniah, Hari Kishen Singh Surjeet and representatives of the PWP and the RSP. Also participating were Chandrajeet Yadav, Raghunath Reddy, K.D. Malaviya, Karpoori Thakur, Shyam Nandan Mishra and Chaudhuri Brahm Prakash. The point to note was that the meeting represented all the elements which were later to provide the support base for the Charan Singh Government. Limaye's move was seen by many as a "projection of a long-nursed dream of the Communist Party of India."

Not to be left behind, George Fernandes called for a separate convention of "all Socialists" in early July. Though this convention expressed dissatisfaction over certain trends in the party, the former president of the Socialist Party, George Fernandes, pointed out that "anyone who broke the unity of the Janata Party might contribute to the return of the dictator."[7]

The "hawks" in the Charan Singh camp were in the meantime breathing down their leader's neck to quit the Government and the party and revive the BLD. But there were also the "doves" around the Jat leader who did not want him to take any more risk. Among them was his powerful Chaudhurani, Gayatri Devi, telling her husband that enough was enough. With what great difficulties his "banwas" (political exile) had ended and now these ruffians of the Raj Narain brigade wanted him to go back into oblivion ! Nothing doing, she said. Charan Singh agreed. Why lose even the Finance Ministry ? Once when he had been a minister under Sucheta Kripalani in Uttar Pradesh, she had given him the portfolio of Forests, perhaps under the impression that he would prefer to quit rather than accept such a minor portfolio. But Charan Singh had taken it, and the joke had gone around that he had been made the "Minister for Rest." A bird in hand was better . . . . No matter how much Raj Narain would press him, he decided, he would stay where he was. And when the "hawks" really got on

[7]Surendra Mohan, Socialist leader, in *Mainstream,* Annual Number, 1979.

his nerves, Charan Singh announced the "final parting of ways" between him and Raj Narain. This was on 3 July, just ten days after Raj Narain resigned from the Janata Party following the Parliamentary Board's decision asking Devi Lal to seek a vote of confidence in the Haryana legislature party. Charan Singh took objection to Raj Narain's statement in a Delhi magazine that it was the Finance Minister who had given him the "idea to resign". "The latest interview," said Charan Singh, "amounts to the last straw. I treat it as the final parting of ways between us." Though he confirmed that Raj Narain had asked him to quit the Janata Party along with him, he said he had refused. "When he (Raj Narain) insisted, I let him do what he wanted."[8] Raj Narain, of course, gave his own interpretation to what Charan Singh had described as a "final parting of ways." He said he could not dissociate himself from Charan Singh as his relations with him were "spiritual and sublime." Devi Lal, too, said that they could not afford to break their relations with Charan Singh and "say goodbye."

Even so, spurned by their leader, Raj Narain and some of his close friends got down to discussing their next move. The Lok Sabha session was only a few days away, and Raj Narain was faced with the prospect of sitting in the House all by himself. It was here that the peculiar characteristic of camaraderie among the old followers of Ram Manohar Lohia came into play. Maniram Bagri, Janata MP and an old friend of Raj Narain, was particularly anxious to save his friend the discomfiture of having to sit alone in the House. He himself had decided to join Raj Narain, but even that would make only two, quite a come-down for a leader who had been threatening to bring the Government tumbling down.

Bagri started approaching his political friends. He also went to B.P. Maurya, with whom he had been close for a long time. "I am caught up in a great dilemma," he told Maurya. "I don't know what I should do. How can we allow Raj Narain to sit alone?"

"You also sit with him," Maurya said.

"That I will," said Bagri, "but what will happen to the party?" Maurya suggested he should go and meet Charan Singh. Bagri went to him, but the old man had burst out, "You people are breaking the party. It is against the interest of the party and the nation. You

---

[8]*The Statesman*, 4 July 1979.

shouldn't do it."

Crestfallen, Bagri returned to Maurya. "Where the hell did you send me ?" he complained to his friend.

Then they all started working together—Bagri, Raj Narain and B.P. Maurya.

The Congress (S) had already been galvanized into action by the Urs-Mrs Gandhi split. They were eager to live down the impression that had been created that they were in cahoots with the Janata leaders. At the Bangalore convention which Urs had called on 4 July, it had been decided that Congressmen would henceforth act on two fronts : in the South, where Mrs Gandhi was stronger, they would work towards demolishing her image and in the North they would work for erosion in the Janata Party. This line of action had been approved even by H.N. Bahuguna who had been approached by some of the former Socialist Forum men in the Congress. But none of them knew how fast events would move.

After Raj Narain announced his resignation from the Janata Party, H.N. Bahuguna goaded Raghunath Reddy and some other Congress (S) men to persuade Y.B. Chavan to move a no-confidence motion against the Government in the Lok Sabha. They knew nothing would come out of the motion, yet it suited the new mood of the Congress (S) which wanted to prove that it had nothing to do with the Janata Party. But this move clashed with Madhu Limaye's plan, which was being executed by Raj Narain. They were still planning to keep the fight confined to their own side. Their calculation was that in the first instance the Government's strength would be reduced to about 267 or so—just a few short of absolute majority. Their plan had been to use the six-week session to systematically damage the image of Morarji Desai and defeat him in a snap censure motion in the last day or two. But the fast-moving events were running away with everybody's calculations.

On 7 July, B.P. Maurya had gone to 12 Willingdon Crescent and had found Mrs Gandhi almost in tears. He had never seen her feeling so low for a long time. "Mauryaji, I don't know what will happen now," she told him. "Urs has left and people tell me you also are about to go . . . . I'll be convicted by the end of October. . . ."[9]

[9] As related by B.P. Maurya in an interview with the author.

"Yes, you'll be convicted," Maurya had told her bluntly, and had left her feeling worse. She had called him again the next day and asked him "to do something."

"Why aren't you supporting the no-confidence motion?" Maurya asked her.

"No, no, that's no good. It may be just good music, but nothing can come of it."

"I don't agree, Madam, you should support it. The Government will fall."

Mrs Gandhi was not willing to believe it. "Are you sure, Mauryaji?" she asked.

"Yes," said Maurya confidently.

She had got interested, and had asked him on what he based his calculations. Maurya gave her the scenario as he saw it and told her that if she were to promise support to Charan Singh the Government would definitely fall.

Anxious to get rid of the Janata Government at any cost, Mrs Gandhi had agreed. Once it was gone, she could take care of the situation as it arose.

"But you'll have to promise one thing, Madam," Maurya had said.

"What ?"

"You will have to promise that you will not be the candidate for Prime Ministership."

Mrs Gandhi had been taken aback by his words, but she had said with great solemnness, "Mauryaji, not only now. . .throughout my life, I say on oath that I am not a candidate for prime ministership. But I should not be humiliated, that's all I want."

"Not only you should not be humiliated, Madam, you should be respected. But you must never think of becoming Prime Minister again."

Mrs Gandhi said : "Mauryaji, I say on oath that I am not a candidate for prime ministership and will never be throughout my life, but only see that this Government is defeated."

By the evening of 8 July, five of Lohiaite MPs had decided to quit the party and join Raj Narain in the House. At this point, Devi Lal went into action. Between him and Maniram Bagri, they were able to get another five MPs to leave on the first day of Parliament session.

When the session began next morning, and Y.B. Chavan sought leave of the House to introduce the censure motion, it got no support from the Congress (I) members. The lady's directive had obviously not reached them yet. It was only some hours later that C.M. Stephen changed the party's stand and announced support for Chavan's motion. But even at that stage, nobody was taking the motion seriously. They thought it was just one of those censure motions which are talked out. That evening B.P. Maurya had again gone to Mrs Gandhi and shown her his list of Janata Party members who would quit. But she was still not willing to believe it. "It's not possible," she said. Maurya's list had the name of George Fernandes and she was not ready to believe that he would quit. She had been told George was going to oppose the motion.

The next day, however, Karpoori Thakur arrived in Delhi and the second batch of defectors from the Janata included as many as nine from Bihar alone. With the number of defectors rising like a river in flood, the political atmosphere was suddenly surcharged and even such of the supporters of Charan Singh who would have preferred to wait and watch a little longer before taking a decision were swept off their feet. Raj Narain, Karpoori Thakur, Devi Lal and others had seen to it that hundreds of Socialist and BLD workers from Bihar and Haryana descended on Delhi to pressurize their representatives to quit the Janata Party. Some of the MPs were virtually besieged and forced to cross the floor.

Charan Singh was watching it all, but he was still hesitant. Maurya had gone and told him that Mrs Gandhi was willing to support him, but he had found it difficult to believe. "She will deceive me," he told Maurya, but the latter told him she had promised on oath to support him. In any case, Charan Singh could see that unless he acted he would lose the support of a sizeable number of his followers, but he would not decide in a rush. By 10 July, the Janata Party's majority had shrunk to three, and Morarji Desai was pressing Charan Singh to defend the Government in the Lok Sabha. In a heated exchange over the telephone, Charan Singh told Desai: "I shall be guided by my followers and do whatever they want me to."[10]

Suddenly the fall of Morarji Desai seemed within the realms of

[10]*The Statesman*, 11 July 1979.

possibility. Already, Babu Jagjivan Ram was building himself up. On 11 July, he called the Janata MPs to his house for a tea party. About 70 of them turned up, but the number given out to the press was 135. By that time the total strength of the party in the Lok Sabha had already come down to 260. The tea party was meant to show that he already commanded a majority in the Janata Party. The ploy was well known; Ram had done this too often in the past for anyone not to know the purpose.

The same evening, the CFD group met and some of Bahuguna's supporters suggested that the group should quit the Janata Party. But Babuji had other ideas. He said it would be "Machiavellian tactics" to cross the floor at that point. He talked about "political morality" and said it lay in going to the polls after resigning from the party. Bahuguna walked out. It was the final (?) parting of ways between them.

On Thursday, 12 July, both Bahuguna and Biju Patnaik met Morarji Desai. The first to go in was Bahuguna, but it turned out to be a rough meeting. Then Biju went in and started off by assuring Desai that he would not leave the party, and that Desai should also try to persuade Bahuguna to stay on. Said Desai : "He (Bahuguna) is the villain of the piece. It is all his doing. After this business is over I'll teach him a lesson." Used to playing the Narad *muni*, Biju at once went and told the story to Bahuguna.

That night Bahuguna, Patnaik and Madhu Limaye met at the house of Chandra Shekhar. They suggested to the party president that the only way to save the Janata Government was to throw out the Jan Sangh. But Chandra Shekhar would have none of it. "You want me to throw out the people who are sitting quietly and to placate those who are defecting ! What sort of logic is this ?" As for himself, Chandra Shekhar had already given word to Desai that in spite of all his differences with him, he would be with him at least till the voting on the censure motion was over.

At the Janata Parliamentary Board meeting the next day, George Fernandes was to put forth the proposal that the Prime Minister should step down. Ram and Vajpayee, it had been decided earlier, would support the move. But Chandra Shekhar had once again refused to be a party to this, saying that he was in politics for "human dignity" and if anybody came up with such a move he would throw the person out of the party. George Fernandes did make the proposal and Babuji nodded his head in assent. Chandra

Shekhar remained quiet. Morarji stuck to his guns : only 47 had so far left the party and the Government could survive even up to 70 defections. That day Bahuguna left the party.

In the night of 14 July, Jagjivan Ram sent off his long letter to Morarji, a virtual indictment of his Government. A copy of it was sent to Chandra Shekhar, another to Bahuguna. Next morning, Bahuguna was in a meeting with some of his supporters and Congress leaders, discussing ways of keeping the CPM from going back to Morarji. It was Bahuguna who had managed to wean away the CPM support, thereby tilting the balance against Desai. He had done this mainly through Surjit Singh, whose real concern was to reinstall Devi Lal in Haryana, perhaps because he had inducted two CPM leaders in his ministry. The meeting was still on when Babuji rang up to say that he had sent his letter to Desai and that it contained all the allegations Bahuguna had made against the Government.

"But the word resignation is not there," Bahuguna said curtly. "That will be done tomorrow," came the reply.

Meanwhile, Ram had gone to Morarji and agreed that the issues raised in the letter would be thrashed out after the censure motion was over. Ram perhaps got the impression that Desai would step down in his favour afterwards, and so he promised to remain in the party and defend it. And yet, the same day after a visit to the Rashtrapati Bhawan, Ram told Chandra Shekhar that he was going to quit the party and the Government. By then he had got feelers from the Congress. Newspapers were already full of reports that he was going to join the Congress. But what eventually gave cold feet to Ram was the fact that while the Congress leadership had welcomed him into their party, they had refused to make any commitment about making him the leader.

By Sunday afternoon, Morarji had got the assessment of his position from people he really trusted, one of them being his Home Minister, H.M. Patel. Even George Fernandes who had waxed eloquent defending the Desai Government on Thursday had deserted that morning. It was no use any more. Desai drove to the Rashtrapati Bhawan and submitted his [resignation to Sanjeeva Reddy.

Following the entire operation with growing delight was Mrs. Gandhi, and watching it closely from his Embassy building on Shanti Path was Peter Y. Strautmanis, Deputy of the USSR.

IX

RETURN OF THE LADY?

From an 'untouchable' of Indian politics, Mrs Gandhi suddenly became the king-maker. In less than a fortnight her fortunes changed beyond her wildest dreams. Until 8 July she had been in the depths of despair, almost certain that she would be prosecuted by October. Her erstwhile henchman, Devaraj Urs had virtually driven her into a corner, and at one go her party had not only lost Karnataka but also the leadership of the Opposition in the Lok Sabha. That had seemed a blow from which it was hard for her to recover. And yet here she was now, holding the country's political balance. So swift had been the change, that every party, every politician, had been left dazed, even Devaraj Urs. He had based all his calculations on two premises—that the Janata Government would somehow drag on for another year or so and that Mrs Gandhi would be in jail by October. Both the premises had gone wrong. He himself had gone into the background, almost as fast as he had got into the national focus. When Y.B. Chavan had decided to move a no-confidence motion in the Lok Sabha, Urs had made a frantic long-distance call to him, telling him to stop it. "Don't upset all my plans," Urs had told Chavan. He was already a little apprehensive of what might happen. Raj Narain had met him in

Bangalore and perhaps he had gauged a bit of his mind, the possibility of his joining hands with Mrs Gandhi and Sanjay. That
surely would ruin all the work he had been doing. But it was
too late; events had gone beyond control, taken a life of their own,
as it were.

It had all started with Morarji's resignation. The President invited
Y.B. Chavan, the 66-year-old man from Satara, to try his hand at
forming a government. Had it been some days earlier, the invitation
would certainly have gone to C.M. Stephen, but Urs had deprived
him of that chance. He had suddenly ceased to be the Opposition
leader. Chavan tried hard for a couple of days but the task proved
too much for him. Simply nobody could form a Government without either the Jan Sangh or the Indira Congress, both political
'untouchables' for many. And in any case, the Jan Sangh was stick-
ing to the Janata Party and Mrs Gandhi had no use for "enemies"
and "traitors" in the Congress. She could not even think of letting
Chavan & Co. have the reins of the Government. As far as she was
concerned, no Congress except her own even existed. Chavan did
send feelers to Charan Singh, but he was itching for the crown himself. This was his last chance and he would not let it go at any cost.
Chavan gave up. But in his letter to the President reporting his
failure, he said that "as a result of our efforts, there has emerged a
combination of parties and groups which to my mind would be able
to provide a viable and stable Government. I trust you will consider
this new situation and deal with it as you in your wisdom deem
proper."

The ball was in Sanjeeva Reddy's court, and many suspected that
he was playing a political game of his own when he called upon
both Charan Singh and Morarji Desai to furnish the evidence of
their claimed majority within 48 hours. Yes, Desai was still around;
even though he had resigned from prime ministership he had made
it clear that he was still the party leader. At the meeting of the
Janata Party executive and parliamentary board where his resignation letter was drafted, H.M. Patel had reminded him to dictate his
letter of resignation from the party leadership too. But Desai had
retorted: "Why should I? I was elected the party leader for five
years and only a two-thirds majority in the parliamentary party can
throw me out of that position." Babu Jagjivan Ram was furious,
but there was little he could do.

The 48 hours set by the President saw the fortunes of the two sides fluctuating by the hour, as though the political scene had turned into one big *satta bazar*. The air was rife with rumours and speculations of all sorts. Some said the President would allow neither to form a government—which many would have welcomed —and others that he would instal a puppet caretaker government, no matter whether the Constitution permitted it or not. Raj Narain had been in almost daily touch with Sanjay Gandhi and the Congress (I) had even formally offered their support to Charan Singh—"unconditional support," they had said at that time. Raj Narain just could not understand what the dilly-dallying of the President was all about. He sought an appointment with the President and conveyed the "mood" of the people : "Blood will flow on the streets of Delhi if Charan Singh is not invited to form the Government." A show of physical strength was already in the offing. With Delhi surrounded by Jat areas, Raj Narain could gather a fanatic army of supporters within 24 hours. But the President, obviously, could not be browbeaten by such talk. He had already talked to the Army, said reporters covering the Rashtrapati Bhawan. It all sounded very ominous, but then suddenly on 26 July word came that the President had invited Charan Singh to form a government. The time was 4.20 p.m.

Whether inadvertently or otherwise, Morarji Desai had committed a "political sin" by sending in a bogus list to the President. He of course had his excuses. He had thought he had been given one more day by the President to submit the list of his supporters. However, on the 25th morning, the President had asked that the list be submitted by 4 p.m. that day. The list was thus submitted "under pressure of time." Desai, nevertheless, felt so penitent that he thought it his "moral duty to atone for the lapse" and announced that he was not only resigning from the Janata Party leadership but also from "active politics."

Charan Singh had at last made it to the chair where he had been dying to be. He thought he could now afford to act high and mighty and spurned suggestions that he should personally go to Mrs Gandhi and thank her for her support. Within hours of his take-over, even Raj Narain was suddenly acting brave. Speaking at a Ramlila Maidan rally, he publicly denigrated Sanjay Gandhi, and his friend, Maniram Bagri, went a step further and described Mrs Gandhi as a "rat" whom they would crush. But perhaps it was only their public faces. Raj Narain returned to his house and immediately telephoned Sanjay Gandhi and begged to be forgiven for the "slip" he had made.

Another big provocation to Mrs Gandhi and Sanjay was the list of Congress ministers to be sworn in. Some of them were "enemies" of the Indira palace and some "turncoats." While the choice of names raised a storm in the Congress (S) itself, Mrs Gandhi made it plain through her mouthpieces that Charan Singh's days were numbered. Ironically, Charan Singh could not even see that he was still surrounded by many of the same people he had earlier considered a 'pack of impotent people'. Indeed, he now headed the team; all the "corrupt" men had suddenly been purified by the Charan touch! As for Jagjivan Ram, his great despair was that he could not even defect to the Congress and become a minister. For the first time in his long political career—except for the brief period when Nehru 'kamarajed' him—he faced the dismal prospect of being out of the Government. Not only a sad but a frightful prospect for a man with cupboards full of skeletons. But now installed as the Opposition leader, he was already putting forth his tentacles, building up new pipelines. He would not rule out the possibility of his meeting with Mrs Gandhi, he told newsmen. The meeting was very much on the cards, whispered his supporters. Why not? It would suit both sides. Mrs Gandhi would forget all about Suresh Kumar and the Jaguar deal and Ram would shut his eyes to all that Sanjay had done. They could come to a wonderful understanding and live happily ever after!

But those who knew Mrs Gandhi better could see that it was all part of her blackmailing tactics. She was out to demolish all her possible contenders one by one, before she was ready for mid-term polls. In the meantime she would make all of them dance around her. Nobody had any doubts about her designs. The Desai Government had proved too much of a nuisance. It had seemed to go on and on, and the arrogant old man had looked like becoming as powerful as she herself had once been. One by one, Desai had worsted his rivals in the party, first Jagjivan Ram and then Charan Singh. Mrs Gandhi had for long been itching to pull the Government down, but she knew it could only be done from inside. Her son had been working on Raj Narain, mainly through their common friend, Kapil Mohan of Mohan Meakin Breweries, but what could that joker do? He had proved too easy an ally, but it had been a painful decision for Mrs Gandhi to agree to support

Charan Singh. She could never have imagined herself doing a thing like this, but she was in desperate straits and there was no other way out. As one of her storm-troopers said, "We had to use one demon to kill the other. Desai is gone, now it will be the turn of Charan Singh."

The Indira Congress had started its tirade against the new coalition even before it was installed. "Do you think we can tolerate a man who called our leader a liar? Just you wait and see what we will do to him." Within a couple of days everybody got a foretaste of what they might do to Charan Singh. Mrs Gandhi's party promptly lent its shoulder to the crumbling ministry of Ram Sunder Das in Bihar, thereby giving a clear ultimatum to the new Prime Minister that he better behave.

Sanjay Gandhi had already told Raj Narain that as a first step towards retaining the support of the Congress (I), the Government would have to withdraw the notification under the Special Courts Act filed in the Supreme Court on 19 July. They would not only have to withdraw the *Kissa Kursi Ka* case, but also remove Ram Jethmalani from the post of special counsel in the case immediately. But Charan Singh seemed out to show his Jat guts. He announced the appointment of H.R. Khanna as the Law Minister, a deliberate defiance flung in Mrs Gandhi's face. Khanna himself resigned a few days later, but even his successor, S.N. Kacker, promptly came out with a defiant statement. No withdrawal of Special Courts, no withdrawal of the KKK case.

Except perhaps Charan Singh who was suddenly in as much of a beatific bliss as Desai had been, nobody gave more than a few months at the outside to the ministry. Not even the newly-sworn Ministers. They were so lacking in confidence that many of them would not even move to the bigger houses meant for ministers. Almost for the first time, there was no scramble for the bungalows, not because the new ministers had no charm for them, but because they were apprehensive of the loss of face they would have to suffer in returning within months to their old flats. Indeed, so fragile was the new Government that many a foreign diplomat in the capital found himself in a quandary. Asked one, rather hesitantly : "Do you think it would be impolitic to send our greetings to the new Government at this stage?" It was only after both Brezhnev and Carter had sent in their good wishes that many of the Delhi-based diplomats followed suit.

The trump card was with the lady at 12 Willingdon Crescent—more precisely with her son—and nobody could tell for sure how it would be played. The courtiers of mother and son only made the confusion worse confounded. Some said she would let the Government go on till November, others said she would pull it down the very day the Lok Sabha opened—on 20 August. It was almost as if they were deliberately talking in two voices in order to keep everybody guessting.

Jagjivan Ram, a much older contender for the crown than Charan Singh, had already made his overtures to the lady and her son. His faithful hanger-on, D.N. Tewari, had been kowtowing to Sanjay Gandhi, and promising that Ram would be willing to pay any price. Ram could never forgive Morarji Desai for having stood in the way of his coveted goal. He had no doubt that if Desai had quit the party leadership on the very first day, he would have mustered enough support to become Prime Minister—even without the lady's help. For days on end, while Desai hung on to the Janata Party leadership, Ram burned with rage : "Come what may I will never allow that Jat to become the Prime Minister."

All he could do was to keep trying. In his broadcast on 29 July, Ram virtually declared that he was going to organize the toppling of the Charan Singh Government and that the President would have no alternative but to call him to form a Government. Suddenly he was talking about norms and ethics in politics, even while he was thinking of nothing but defections to his side. In a TV appearance which did no good to his image, Ram huffed and puffed about the "recent developments which are not very edifying either to the democratic traditions or to the normal ethical standards. . ." Democracy and ethical standards, as one political commentator put it, were safe only as long as Babuji was "securely fixed to a ministerial chair!"

In an effort to confuse everybody, Jagjivan Ram got a resolution passed by the party National Executive, which said that anyone believing in either a Hindu or a Muslim State would not be allowed to be a member of the Janata Party. This was his clever ploy to get over the nagging question of dual membership; he thought the resolution would make it easier to get defectors from other parties. But even while he was doing his best to gobble up any MPs he could, he was all the time waiting for a word from the lady. Wouldn't she prefer him to Charan Singh? But there were analysts who argued that Mrs Gandhi would never allow a situation in which Ram could become the Prime Minister. Her eyes were obviously fixed on the next elections, and the main support base that she could hope for was a combination of the upper castes, the Harijans and the minorities. If she could keep that combination in her hold, she could gain a majority in the Lok Sabha. And until that time Ram enjoyed only a marginal support of the Harijans, but her camp was not at all sure if the situation would remain the same if he were allowed to become the Prime Minister. Wouldn't he then be able to consolidate the Harijan votes in the country?

The argument was not without its logic, but the other alternative did not seem much better for her. Ranged behind Charan Singh were not only the ten million Jats spread over Punjab, Haryana, Rajasthan and Uttar Pradesh, but a whole combination of a long-subdued middle castes all over the country. With him were all the populist leaders of the Yadavas, the Ahirs, the Koeris, the Kurmis, the Hajjams and the rest of them. Their vaulting ambitions had reached a point of militancy, as had been so clearly in evidence at the Kisan Rally in December 1978. There you had Karpoori Thakur, one of the symbols of the new-found Backward Class power, giving notice to the country: "The kisans will demand no more, they will take." The cocky plumes of the pugrees of Karpoori Thakur, Devi Lal and Ram Naresh Yadav had heralded the new power structure that had come into being. If Mrs Gandhi was flaunting herself as the champion of the downtrodden Harijans and the minorities, Charan Singh was being hailed as the Messiah of the country's rising middle castes. As Pradhan H. Prasad, one of the most perceptive analysts of the country's socio-economic scene, pointed out :

The middle caste Hindus in North India remain a formidable lot. They account for about 36 per cent of the population. They outnumber upper caste Hindus by about 55 per cent. The traditional dominance of upper caste Hindus is being undermined by the increasing economic power of the middle castes. The dice, therefore, would seem to be loaded in favour of the middle castes...The working of our democracy has already broken the monolith of semi-feudal power in North India. This is a healthy sign...the disintegration of semi-feudal agrarian relations which operate as a drag on the rapid development of agriculture is in sight. As the intensity of struggle touches new heights, there will be further realignments and adjustments....[1]

Even as it was, the forces ranged behind Charan Singh were at least an equal match to Mrs Gandhi in the States which could make or mar her future. But now that Charan Singh had become the Prime Minister of a coalition consisting of the Congress, the CFD and the Socialists (if only the splinters of the last two), he would be in a far better position to extend his base among the middle castes in the South. Devaraj Urs, who had himself risen by consolidating the middle castes in his State, could certainly take care of that. And what could be even more upsetting to Mrs Gandhi was the presence of H.N. Bahuguna on Charan's side, for whatever else one might say of the man, he did have some popular base among the Muslims of Uttar Pradesh. Besides, he was one of the smoothest political operators, especially in electoral politics, as Mrs Gandhi knew so well. Certainly, she would never want the Charan Singh-Bahuguna combination to last for any length of time, at least not in the Government. Together they were quite capable of upsetting her electoral calculations in the vital States of the North.

But as it happened, it was not so much these considerations which led to the withdrawal of Mrs Gandhi's support to Charan Singh. The *casus belli* was Charan Singh's refusal to bail out Sanjay Gandhi from his immediate legal problems. A couple of days before Charan Singh was scheduled to seek a vote of confidence, Sanjay Gandhi warned Raj Narain that if he wanted the Charan Government to continue, he must get his demands accepted. Straight from the Mohan Meakin Guest House where the two met, under the usual cover of a religious ceremony, Raj Narain had rushed to Charan Singh and from there to Biju Patnaik's house. There they called an important member of the Congress (I) for consultations. The talks merely confirmed the position: either Sanjay Gandhi's demands were met or the Congress(I) support would go. Raj Narain rushed back to Charan Singh and explained the situation to him. Charan Singh called the Law Minister, S.N. Kacker, and asked him to see if something could be done about the *Kissa Kursi Ka* case. After full consultations with high officials of his ministry, Kacker gave a Note to the Prime Minister: "...On 7 June, 1979, Law Ministry finalised the draft of declaration to be issued under Section 5(1) of the Special Courts

[1]In *Mainstream*, 25 August 1979.

Act. (On) 22.6.79 declaration under Section 5(1) of the Act made. The declaration, inter alia, recites that the Central Government after fully and carefully examining the material placed before it in regard to the aforesaid offences is of the opinion that there is prima facie offence...On July 19 the declaration was filed in Supreme Court under Section 7 of the Special Courts Act. The transfer of the appeals from High Court to Supreme Court had to be automatic; the words being 'shall stand transferred.' *It is not possible to withdraw the aforesaid notification in view of the aforesaid facts and circumstances. Withdrawal of the notification at this stage would expose us to ridicule.* Shri Ram Jethmalani was appointed as a Special Counsel by the previous Government. The implication of removing him from that assignment may be considered because it is certain that this would be criticised as the *first step towards soft-pedalling.*" (Italics mine).

Charan Singh said he would prefer to resign rather than give in to the blackmail of Sanjay Gandhi. An angry Raj Narain stalked out of the room, saying, "This Jat will never understand anything!"

When the Lok Sabha met on 20 August, Charan Singh announced that his Government was resigning and he was going to the President to recommend the dissolution of the House. He had sat barely for 35 seconds in the Prime Minister's seat! After two days, packed with wild rumours and conjectures, came the brief communique from the Rashtrapati Bhawan : "In exercise of the powers conferred upon me by sub-clause (b) of clause (2) of Article 85 of the Constitution, I hereby dissolve the Lok Sabha." An opinion poll carried out by *India Today* said a majority of the people were in agreement with the President's decision. The replies to the question if they wanted a mid-term poll were: Yes—75% urban, 63% rural; No—21% urban and 20% rural; Don't Know—16% urban and 5% rural. Indeed after all the unseemly happenings since 9 July, there was hardly much choice left for Sanjeeva Reddy, notwithstanding all the holes that the partisans could pick in his decision. In fact, by allowing Charan Singh to have formed a Government at all, the President had given ground to the Janata leaders under Jagjivan Ram to raise a hue and cry. There was little doubt that Sanjeeva Reddy had discriminated between two groups of defectors: the one which had gone along with Charan Singh and the other which Jagjivan Ram hoped to get. Even while he was meeting the representatives of the two sides, the President's mind was already made up.

That was evident from the well-authenticated dialogue that took place during the last meeting between President Reddy and the Janata leaders on the morning of 22 August. About the first thing that Reddy did was to show Jagjivan Ram and Chandra Shekhar a letter which C.M. Stephen and Dr Chenna Reddy had brought from Mrs Gandhi. It was a letter of consent to the President's proposal to name Surjit Singh Barnala as the head of an interim Government. As was known, Reddy had earlier toyed with the names of Sheikh Abdullah and Hidayatullah, but this Barnala idea was quite a shock for the Janata leaders.

"How can you do this when I am quite sure of a majority?" Ram had protested indignantly.

"You seem to be depending on defectors," the President remarked.

"But you have made a defector the Prime Minister," retorted Ram.

"That was not a defection," said the President, "that was a revolt."

It was perhaps only to cushion the blow that President Reddy asked Ram to go ahead and submit a list of supporters in order to prove his majority.

But Ram said: "I'll prove my majority on the floor of the House."

The President would not agree to that, and the meeting ended rather abruptly, with Chandra Shekhar saying, "All right, we'll meet you tomorrow."

Within an hour or so, Charan Singh had been called to head a caretaker Government.

Indira lao, desh ko bachao goes the cry of her cheer-leaders. Once again "stability" and "order" would be the catchwords of Mrs Gandhi. Even in 1971, the walls of cities and towns were plastered over with posters of the lady "standing between order and chaos." After all the nauseating political spectacle that the country recently witnessed, the slogan would go down well with quite a few sections of people in the country—all the get-rich-quick men, all the industrial and business houses, all the sick Hindu middle class of this country which craves for a charismatic leader who would keep them under leash, all of them would lap up her slogan. According to one of the many theories on the Indian political ethos going around, the country had been oscillating between authoritarianism and freedom and this time the people were all waiting to run after a dictator, even a tinpot dictator. As the British writer Maurice Latey pointed out,[2] the legacy of tyranny even after its fall was a dangerous one. In Rome the delusion that the infamous Nero had returned from the grave was welcomed by the populace and the French people, exasperated by the bumbling incompetence and lack of glamour of democratic governments, had craved the glory and excitement of Napoleon. It has been usual for dictators to get the reputation, often undeserved, of the efficient man/woman who "gets things done"—

> It is scarcely imaginable that men anywhere should remember Hitler's autobahns and abolition of unemployment and forget the gas chambers and holocausts of war. But which of us, frustrated by the inefficiency and muddle and unnecessary contention of government by consent, has not on occasion thought: 'What could not I do, if I had dictatorial powers? The problems are all so simple. Just remove a few crooks and incompetents. Oh no! No question of concentration camps or secret police, let alone gas chambers or nuclear bombs.' Yet it only needs enough people to think that way at the same time for long enough and with sufficient ferocity, and that is where it would lead.[3]

The fantastic campaigner that Mrs Gandhi is, she is bound to make the most of the dismal administrative record of the Janata Government, its mutual contradictions and endless wranglings, its failure to come to grips with the vital problems of the economy, its failure to create any confidence among the minorities and the poor sections of society. Mrs Gandhi will be projecting herself as the saviour of the Muslims and the Harijans, as the only leader who can hold the country together, the only one who can give the country stability, never mind if it is the stability of a graveyard. None of these claims is new. In fact, one has never heard a single campaign speech of Mrs Gandhi in which she has forgotten to touch

[2]In *Tyranny—A Study in the Alu:e of Power*.
[3]*Ibid.*

on these points, but this time she is going to rub them in hard—and
with good effect, for alas, public memory is so short! She will talk
long and hard about Belchi and Bajitpur and one can take a safe
wager that not one of her campaign speeches will ever miss out
Jamshedpur, Aligarh, Hyderabad, Sambhal and all the other places
which have been affected during the last 28 months. And when
she speaks about all these she will be hoping that everybody
would have forgotten all about the atrocities on Harijans and all
about the communal riots during her "glorious decade" and nobody
would ever remember Muzaffarnager or Turkman Gate. She would
of course gloss over the fact that more atrocities on Harijans took
place between 1974 and 1977 (June) than in the years of the Janata
rule, as established in a study based on data compiled by the
National Integration Division of the Union Government on the
reports sent by State Governments and by the Intelligence Bureau.
Perhaps she would say that all of that had been more than made
up by her elephant ride to Belchi!

One of Mrs Gandhi's most effective weapons against her rivals
has been the rhetoric of ideology. She has always been able to show
up her opponents as "reactionary," while assuming for herself the
image of a great champion of the poor and the oppressed. She has
done it ever since she first split the Congress in 1969. Like Hitler,
all would-be dictators swear by democracy and "socialism" to
acquire power. "Whenever Mrs Gandhi is in difficulty," Brahmanand
Reddi once remarked, "she talks of socialism. Who reduced the
quantum of bonus for workers from 8.33% to 4%?"[4] When Mrs
Gandhi visited Wales in October 1978 to open her industrialist
friend's steel mill, she talked volubly about her faith in democracy,
but qualified it by the "needs of the people." Rhetorically she had
asked: "What is important—the needs of the people or the voice of
the people or the privileges of the few? This is the problem facing
India. If the poor felt at any time that the system was not meeting
their needs, would they tolerate the system? This is the question to
which we have to find an answer. . ." As S. Nihal Singh pointed
out, what Mrs Gandhi had to offer to the country was a mixture
of populism and strong-arm methods with no deeper philosophy to
guide her than her self-aggrandisement.

And yet, even her worst critics would agree, Mrs Gandhi has

many plus points. She is certainly the most charming, the most sophisticated leader in the country. There is nobody who can beat her in sweetness when she wishes to be sweet. She is not an ordinary person, one is told so often. "She is the daughter of Jawaharlal Nehru." The very fact that the obvious is repeated implies that you cannot put her at par with the others. In fact, she is not a mere politician, she is something of a queen, and in a country with such long traditions of rajas and ranis, even to the extent that few stories of childhood begin without a raja or a rani and their sons and daughters, Mrs Gandhi gets a tremendous advantage over all the others. "This is where Mrs Gandhi wins even before going into battle," wrote Sasthi Brata. "Her strongest political card is that she believes neither in democracy nor in truth. Instead she is driven by a pathological conviction in the synonomity between her personal rule and the good of the nation. Unhampered by the constraints that a cultured and civilized education imposes upon a rapacious ego, she sees nothing wrong in assuming that the fate of India rests in the hands of the Nehru family..." Indeed, Mrs Gandhi and Sanjay and the Nehrus in general can be forgiven if they think they have been born to rule, because there are thousands of people in this country who genuinely believe there is something superhuman about the Nehru dynasty. Amid all the jubilation over the fall of the Congress in 1977, there were so many people in this country who were stricken with grief at the personal defeat of Mrs Gandhi, as though a goddess had gone down to a minor demon!

A big plus point for Mrs Gandhi, which many psychologists and poll pundits would forget to take into account, is the widespread sympathy for Mrs Gandhi in distress. It is like the sympathy for a queen in exile, a queen harried and harassed by her own people. This sympathy would win her quite a good number of votes all over India, for she is undoubtedly the only political personality whose following, small or big, runs throughout the length and breadth of the country. It is sad but true that no other single leader has a personal following, whatever the reasons for it, as large as Mrs Gandhi's. Her advantages by no means end there. In sheer campaigning the lady has no peers. She can go on and on when people half her age would pass out with sheer fatigue. Mrs Gandhi, who was once thought to be too frail and week, even by her aunt Vijayalakshmi Pandit, for the rough and tumble of politics, has already put even the tough males in politics to shame. In the time that Charan Singh or Y.B. Chavan or Jagjivan Ram or even younger men like Chandra Shekhar would address a dozen meetings in five miles, Mrs Gandhi would have done at least 25 meetings over 50 miles. Anybody who followed her campaign trail in Azamgarh during the blistering summer of 1978 would know what I mean. She is unbeatable at that sort of thing. As one reporter recalled, in roughly 48 hours she slept no more than three or four. It was May —UP at its worst. But she had just gone on and on like an inexhaustible dynamo. Besides, she was certainly the biggest crowd collector. Where 15 or 20 thousand people could turn up just to see her face, it would often take days of preparation to collect a similar crowd for most other leaders. Not all the crowds who go to see her cast their vote for her, but they do help in creating an atmosphere.

Atmosphere is a very important part of any election. The very day the House was dissolved and mid-term polls announced, her supporters were going around predicting a clean sweep for her, with even the tantriks and astrologers chipping in their bits. The latter, of course, had their astral signs to read, but if you asked the politicians on what they based their forecasts, they would more often than not say it was their "gut feeling." The talk about her coming back was not only creating an atmosphere but also demoralizing those opposed to her. Undoubtedly, most of Mrs Gandhi's political opponents were frightened people, if one could see beyond the bold front they put up.

But with all her advantages, even her closest of supporters admitted that she would have many hurdles to reckon with. This would be the first time in her political career when she would be fighting a country-wide election without the government machinery at her command. It was one thing to beat all the others in a bye-election, even without all the facilities that go with power, but to campaign all over the country without the helicopters and the air force planes that she had been used to would be a different matter. Not that this would be an insurmountable problem for her, with all the legendary resources at her command, but it would definitely cramp her campaign style to some extent—alas, even in Karnataka this time.

Mrs Gandhi's biggest problem would be her men. Not only was she finding it hard to find the right candidates for the elections, she did not even have one leader worth the name who could share the campaign burden with her. Her party is nothing if you take away the "I" from it. Over the years, she has virtually been left with only the family and their hangers-on, petty politicians who had no strength of their own and so could offer no threat to her or to Sanjay. In the States which would really determine the outcome of the elections, she has nobody with her except the Mishras and the Pandes and the Tripathis and Dixits. Indeed, as a journalist once pointed out, the list of her political supporters in UP and Bihar read more like a directory of Brahmins. That was certainly going to be one of the biggest drawbacks of her party—the predominance of discredited pettifogging Brahmins who could not enthuse even a small section of the electorate in the vital States of North India. Most of the so-called leaders in the Congress (I) were hanging on to her for no better reason than that they were partners in her Emergency crimes. Whether it was Jagannath Mishra or Narayan Dutt Tewari or V.C. Shukla or Bansi Lal, they were all there because they had no choice. When it comes to getting votes for her, they could be of little use, particularly this time.

The mid-term polls would undoubtedly be very different from any other elections before, certainly very different from the one in 1977 when the votes cut across all the known barriers of caste and class and party and became a one-sided affair in most States of the country. It appears, at least at the time of writing, that the elections would once again revert to more mundane factors, except that this time the contenders would have to reckon with factors and combinations which did not exist before. Whether for good or bad, caste and class would come into play in a much more aggravated form this time than ever before.

The South and the North are once again likely to present different pictures. One often hears the general statement that the "South belongs to Mrs Gandhi." True, the South, generally speaking, remained out of the Janata ambit, even in 1977, and it was Mrs Gandhi's great performance in the 1978 Assembly elections in Andhra Pradesh and Karnataka which gave a new spurt to her come-back drive. Let us assume that she sweeps Andhra Pradesh in the coming polls and wins a clear majority in Karnataka in spite of Devaraj Urs. But these are not all there is to the South. What about Kerala and Tamil Nadu? In Kerala, it would appear that she could even end up with a blank, and in Tamil Nadu, in spite of her alliance with the DMK and the people scrambling to have a view of her, it would be considered a good performance if she won seven of the 39 seats in the State. Which is to say that even if her party gets 37 of the 42 seats in Andhra Pradesh (which would by no means be a certainty if the CPI, the CPM and Vengal Rao join hands), and another 16 out of 28 in Karnataka, she would have no more than 60 seats in the South. With all the frustrated and panicky Congressmen of Maharashtra crawling back to her fold and her known strength in Vidharbha and the Marathwada regions, Mrs Gandhi can perhaps hope to get around half of the 48 seats in the State. In Gujarat, which has 26 seats, she has influential leaders like Jinabhai Darji, Madhav Singh Solanki and Sanat Mehta, and she would certainly do well in some parts of the State, especially in the tribal areas in the north. But even her most ardent supporters in Gujarat do not give her more than 16 seats at the outside, and the more objective poll-watchers would not go beyond 12 seats for her party. Let us say she gets 13 in Gujarat, which would mean a total of 37 seats for the two States. The grand total so far: 97.

And so we are back to the well-known position that the Congress (I) or whichever party wants to get absolute majority in the Lok Sabha cannot do so without achieving good results in the northern States, especially in Uttar Pradesh and Bihar which between the two of them have more seats than all the four southern States taken together. UP, Bihar, Madhya Pradesh, Rajasthan, Delhi, Punjab, Haryana and Himachal Pradesh together accont for 238 of the 544 Lok Sabha Seats. In MP, which had become a stronghold of the Jan Sangh, it would almost be a straight fight between Mrs Gandhi's party and the Janata, and it would be surprising if she can go beyond a dozen of the 40 seats. In Rajasthan, too, the Jan Sangh is strongly entrenched, but here the backward-oriented Janata (S) would be able to give a good fight to the Janata. Both the Congress (I) and the Janata would be heavily dependent on the upper castes and would cut into each other's votes. On the other hand the Janata (S) would erode the Harijan and the Muslim votes of the Congress (I) to some extent. While the chances are that the Janata would still come out with the largest number in Rajasthan, thanks to the big increase in the RSS cadre in the State and the Jan Sangh hold on the official machine, the Janata (S) and Congress alliance could capitalize on the resurgent backward votes. Mrs Gandhi ought to be happy if she got six of the 25 seats in the State.

In Punjab (13 seats), the split in the Akali Dal over the question of alliance with the Janata (S)-Congress-CPI front, could give Mrs

Gandhi three to four seats. Haryana could give her no more than two and Himachal Pradesh perhaps none. If there was any pro-Mrs Gandhi breeze anywhere it was for some peculiar reason in Delhi, and by all accounts she had a good chance of winning at least four of the seven seats.

And now to the decisive battlefields of Bihar and Uttar Pradesh. In 1971, when Mrs Gandhi was at the height of her glory, she polled just about 40% of the votes in Bihar but carried away 39 of the 54 seats. In Uttar Pradesh she polled 48.57% of the votes and won 73 of the 85 seats. Her primary vote banks in these two States were the upper castes, the Harijans and the Muslims, but she had got a good chunk of the backward votes as well.

Though it is almost impossible to get an accurate break-up of the various caste groups in any of the States nowadays, the following is the closest one could get to the picture in Bihar:[5]

Category	Caste group	Percentage of total Population
Upper castes	Brahmin	4.7
	Bhumihar	2.9
	Rajput	4.2
	Kayastha	1.2
	Banias	0.6
	Total	13.6
Middle castes	Yadav	11.0
	Kurmi	3.6
	Koeri	4.1
	Barhi	1.0
	Dhanuk	1.8
	Kahar	1.7
	Kandu	1.6
	Kumhar	1.3
	Lohar	1.3
	Mallah	1.5
	Nai (Hajjam)	1.4

[5]Source: For Muslims, Scheduled Castes and Scheduled Tribes, Government of India (1965). For all others, Government of India (1932). The older figures have been adjusted for boundary changes after 1932.

Tatwa		1.6
Teli		2.8
Other backwards		16.0
	Total	50.7
Muslims		12.5
Scheduled Castes (Harijans)		14.1
Scheduled Tribes		9.1

As is clear from the chart, the middle castes constitute the biggest chuuk of the population in Bihar. The position is somewhat different in Uttar Pradesh where the middle castes comprise about 35% of the population and the upper castes about 25%. For the very first time, Mrs Gandhi would have to reckon with the consolidation of middle castes in both the States, particularly in Bihar where they have become an aggressive force under the leadership of Karpoori Thakur, who is himself a hajjam. Together with Ramlakhan Singh Yadav of the Congress, who is the undisputed leader of the Yadavas in Bihar, Thakur would do his utmost to mobilize the maximum percentage of middle caste votes in favour of the Lok-Dal-Congress alliance. At the heart of the Bihar situation is the simple fact that the upper castes who had lorded it over the State for decades have finally lost the battle. Political power has passed, almost irrevocably, into the hands of the backward or middle castes. During the time when the agitation over the reservation of jobs for backwards raged in Bihar, there was not a single political party, not a single organisation in the State which was not vertically split over the issue. And not even the most fanatic opponents of 'reservation' had the courage to oppose it in principle.

The consolidation of the middle castes and their aggressive awareness of strength has not come about suddenly. It is the result of a historical process which has been going on for decades. The gradual decline in the voting percentage of the Congress from 1952 to 1967 had much to do with the gradual coming up of the middle castes, which had first found a platform in the Lohia-led Samyukta Socialist Party, which emerged as the largest single party in the Bihar Assembly elections of 1967. Indeed, the emergence of Charan Singh himself, from a tehsil level politician in the early fifties to the Chief ministership in 1967 and prime ministership in 1979, is to a large extent the result of the growing power of the middle castes in northern India. The process could be traced back to the days of the

Second World War when food prices registered a sudden rise and considerably reduced the burden of land revenue. The income of the middle castes, who were mostly agriculturists, rose. Slowly and steadily they retrieved their long-mortgaged lands from the Thakurs and the Bhumihars who formed the bulk of the absentee landlords and who were increasingly busy sharing the political and administrative plums left by the Britishers. The ruling elites did their best to keep the middle castes out of political and administrative offices, but they could not go on doing it for ever. Adult franchise and the virtual explosion in education were to prove their biggest enemies. The representation of the middle castes in Parliament and State legislatures rose from election to election (the approximate percen-tage for the Lok Sabha are : 22.4% in 1952-57; 29.1% in 1957-62; 27.4% in 1962-67; 30.6% in 1967-71; 33.2% in 1971-77 and 36% in 1977-79). And over the years, the middle castes felt a growing alienation from the Congress Party which had seemed inalienably wedded to protecting the interests of the elites.

What would be particularly disastrous for Mrs Gandhi in Bihar and Uttar Pradesh is a division of Harijan and Muslim votes. In Bihar, Karpoori Thakur had already succeeded during his chief ministership in winning over the "backward Muslims" and some sections of the Harijans. If his alliance could retain the support of even 20% of the Harijans and 25% of the Muslims, it would romp home with at least 25 of the 54 seats in Bihar. What made the situation even worse for Mrs Gandhi in Bihar was the denial of a chance to Jagjivan Ram to become Prime Minister. That won him the sympathy of wide sections of Harijans, especially Chamars, in various parts of the country. And so, if Jagjivan Ram's party cut into the Harijan votes in the northern States to any sizable extent, Mrs Gandhi's prospects could be badly affected. The Muslim votes in Bihar and UP could play an even more crucial role. It was not for nothing that Mrs Gandhi became suddenly critical of the Ram Sunder Das Government in Bihar, soon after she had gone out of her way to save it. The support her party gave to the Das Ministry had clearly antagonised the Muslims in the State. And then with another flare-up in Jamshedpur, the Congress (I) was finding it hard to go on blaming the RSS while it supported the Government of which the Jan Sangh was an integral part. Mrs Gandhi would clearly have to work overtime to retain her traditional vote banks.

Even a dispassionate analysis of Mrs Gandhi's poll prospects would thus seem to throw cold water on all the great enthusiasm of people already proclaiming the "Return of the Lady."

But never say never in politics, specially in politics of the kind we have in India today. Even if Mrs Gandhi falls far short of a majority, as she is likely to, she is quite capable of manoevring her way into power. The lack of convictions and principles on all sides gives her the ideal milieu to function in. What is more important is that the people remember what she and her son stand for, what they have done to the country before and what they will do if they come back.

The "norms and principles" that Mrs Gandhi and her son stand for are enshrined in the findings of Justice Shah. Here are only some gleanings:

Misuse of powers and institution of false criminal complaints against four senior officials by the CBI at the instance of Smt. Indira Gandhi: The evidence discloses a gross abuse of the authority vested in Smt. Indira Gandhi. She had taken into her head to act as she did merely because the officers of the Commerce and Industries Ministries had, in the discharge of their duties taken steps to acquire information which was likely to affect the interest of Maruti Limited. She pressurised Shri D. Sen to take proceedings for searching their houses and for filing complaints against them under the Prevention of Corruption Act, which were wholly unjustified and which were eventually dropped. (Para 7.96)

Smt. Gandhi was responsible for institution of criminal proceedings against the four officers concerned, having their houses searched and subjecting them to humiliation. (Para 7.102)

Unlawful detention of Textile/Customs employees under MISA by Delhi Administration and institution of false CBI cases against four of them: The Commission feels that Smt. Gandhi has abused her authority and misused her power in having caused the arrest and detention of these 12 officers without adequate justification and using the CBI to set in motion criminal cases against four of them, all of which had to be abandoned eventually for want of any material. (Para 7.134)

Deviation from established procedure, misuse of power and abuse of authority by Shri T. R. Tuli, Chairman of the Punjab National Bank in allowing a clean overdraft to M/s Associated Journals Ltd. (*publishers of National Herald*):...No precautions which would be normal in advancing money on clean overdraft account were taken; but solely because of the intervention of the Minister P.C. Sethi loan was advanced disregarding the cannons which would ordinarily govern the advancing of such a loan. (Para 7.156)

Decision Process leading to the purchase of three Boeing 737 Aircraft by Indian Airlines : ...The visit of Shri Rajiv Gandhi to the office of the Chairman of the Indian Airlines, where he was shown the financial projections by the Director of Finance, apparently under the instructions of the Chairman, was a procedure which was totally outside the ordinary course of business... (Para 7.202)

Detention of Shri Bhim Sen Sachar and seven others : The decision was taken by Smt. Gandhi. She had abused her position and misused her power. . . (Para 7.250)

Import of aircraft by Dhirendra Brahmachari of Aparna Ashram: Brahmachari has fully exploited his association with the then Prime Minister's house in getting the aircraft imported by misrepresenting it as a gift. (Para 10.58)

Arrests and detentions : Smt. Indira Gandhi was responsible for directing the arrest and detention of a number of respected citizens without authority of law, motivated solely by a desire to continue to remain in power. (Para 11.79)

Requisition of Vishva Yuvak Kendra, Chanakyapuri, New Delhi under the DISIR Act: The building was requisitioned at the instance of Smt. Indira Gandhi, in order to pressurize the management of the Indian Youth Centre Trust to reconstitute the Board of Trustees. . . (Para 12.13)

Harassment of the firm Messrs. Pandit Brothers; their arrest and related matters: Series of harassments against the firm. . .was intitiated at the instance of Shri Sanjay Gandhi. (Para 12.60)

Shri Sanjay Gandhi who wielded such enormous power during the Emergency did not confine his activities only to the operation of demolition of houses, shops and industrial buildings. . .On the direct responsibility of Shri Sanjay Gandhi for the harassment that was meted out to Pandit Brothers, the Commission feel no doubt. (Para 12.71)

In the view of the Commission the manner in which Shri Sanjay Gandhi functioned in the public affairs of Delhi in particular is the single greatest act of excess committed during the period of Emergency for which there is no parallel nor any justification for such assumption of authority or power in the history of independent India. While the other acts of the excesses may have been in the nature of acts committed by functionaries having some shadow of authority acting in excess of their powers, here was a case of an individual wielding unlimited powers in a dictatorial manner without even the slightest right to it. *If this country is to be rendered safe for future generations, the people owe it to themselves to ensure that an irresponsible and unconstitutional centre of power like the one which revolved round Shri Sanjay Gandhi during the Emergency is not allowed to come up ever again in any form or shape or under any guise.* (Para 13.311)

Turkman Gate firing: Shri Sanjay Gandhi intervened on behalf of Shri Bhinder and pressurized the District Magistrate and his colleagues and a junior magistrate to sign and pre-date the firing order. (Para 14.178)

Observations of the Commission:. . .The circumstances in which the Emergency was declared and the ease with which it was accomplished should be a warning to the citizens of the country. Smt. Indira Gandhi did not consult the Cabinet even though she had plenty of time to do so. There is enough evidence to show that Smt. Indira Gandhi planned the imposition of the Emergency at least as early as June 22. . .the inference is inevitable that a political decision was taken by an interested Prime Minister in a desperate endeavour to save herself from the legitimate compulsion of a judicial verdict against her. (Para 15.5)

The nation owes it to the present and the succeeding generations to ensure that the administrative set up is not subverted in future in the manner it was done to serve the personal ends of any one individual or a group of individuals in or near the Government. (Para 15.6)

Censorship of news and the manner in which the media was manipulated should be a lesson to the Government and to the people that in a vast country like ours blanketing of news in the way it was done has serious repercussions on the lives and thoughts of the people. (Para 15.7)

The Government has a special responsibility to ensure that extra-constitutional centres of power are not allowed to grow and if and when located, to *snuff them out ruthlessly.* (Para 15.21)

But Mrs Gandhi would have us believe that all she and her son did was for the good of the people and the country. She had the effrontery to tell the Shah Commission that when she declared the Emergency the situation in India was similar to the one that "prevailed in France when de Gaulle came to power in 1958."[6] Her literary agents are already saying that the same situation exists once again. She is being hailed as "taller than de Gaulle"—the only one who can set things right!

How does one describe the lady? It is debatable whether she can be put in the category of tyrants. According to one definition of the word, a tyrant is "a ruler who exercises power beyond the scope permitted by the laws, customs and standards of his time and society and who does so with a view to maintaining or increasing that power."[7] The cap certainly fits her.

But not once has she shown any remorse for her actions. Instead, she has imperiously dubbed all the findings against her and Sanjay as "political propaganda." What is worse, she has gone around saying condescendingly that if she came back to power she would not be vindictive towards anybody, that she will be nice and kind to friends and foes alike. How very benign and democratic! It was Adolf Hitler who said that no nation will let its finger be burnt twice. "The trick of the Pied Piper of Hamelin catches people only once." One can only hope he was right.

[6] In her letter to Justice Shah, dated 21 November 1977.
[7] Maurice Latey in *Tyranny—A Study in the Abuse of Power*.